James Martin's

GREAT BRITISH WINTER COOKBOOK

Photography by Simon Wheeler

James Martin's

GREAT BRITISH
WINTER
COOKBOOK

MITCHELL BEAZLEY

*For my mother, grandmother, Ken Allinson, Fiona,
Linda and Mary*

Great British Winter by James Martin

First published in Great Britain in 2006 by Mitchell Beazley, an imprint of
Octopus Publishing Group Ltd, 2-4 Heron Quays, London E14 4JP

Reprinted 2006 (twice)

A CIP catalogue record for this book is available from the British Library.

ISBN 10: 1-84533-040-4
ISBN 13: 978-1-845330-40-8

Commissioning Editor: Rebecca Spry
Executive Art Editor: Nicky Collings
Design: Grade Design Consultants
Editor: Susan Fleming
Photography: Simon Wheeler
Home Economy: Katherine Ibbs and Karen Taylor
Production: Jane Rogers

Typeset in Foundry Sans
Printed and bound in Italy

CONTENTS

Introduction   6

Starters   8

Meat and Game Birds   24

Vegetables   42

Puds   56

Tarts   74

Hallowe'en and Bonfire Night   86

Christmas Baking   104

Christmas Day   118

New Year's Day   140

Parties, Gifts and Treats   152

Index   172

Introduction

THE MAGIC OF CHRISTMAS takes hold of us as kids and never really leaves us. But as a chef, the real magic of winter for me now lies in the food we eat. Salty baked potatoes, warming winter stews, comforting roast beef with Yorkshire pud – you can't beat it! It's not that those winter festivals like Bonfire Night and New Year's Eve have lost their power to excite me, it's just that the thing I like best about them is the food.

Pretty much everything in this book is seasonal, because the joy of having seasons is cooking different ingredients and different types of dishes. So you'll find all your cold-weather favourites like pumpkins, parsnips and potatoes; cod and mussels; pheasant, goose and beef. But for us Brits the winter is also about occasion. Remember the burgers, toffee apples and toasted marshmallows you used to eat on Bonfire Night? Or the sausage rolls and mulled wine you associate with winter parties? It's all in here! I admit that not everything is traditionally British – I've included lots of dishes that we've adopted from abroad over the years.

Of course there's one festivity that's more important than any other in winter. Yes, I'm talking about Christmas. You'll find all your festive favourites in this book, from a couple of alternatives for the roast bird, to the roast potatoes and parsnips, to the bread sauce and cranberry jelly. And there are loads of vegetarian ideas, too! For those of you who fancy indulging in Christmas baking, there are all the recipes you need – the cake, the pudding, the yule log... even traditional mincemeat.

You know I hate the idea of everyone slogging away over a hot stove, so all the food in this book is simple. Happy winter and happy festivities!

STARTERS

Nothing beats a good British soup in the winter. There are loads of fresh ingredients in season, and I particularly love mussels and root veg as a base for soup. But there's nothing wrong with buying some veg frozen – after all, why go without a food like peas for months when it can be frozen so well? Salads make another brilliant winter starter; they're not just for summer, as my recipes prove!

Bacon and Bean Salad

The dressing is the key to this delicious salad. Its texture is a bit like that of a Caesar salad, but less creamy and heavy. It's a pain to remove the shells of broad beans, but it will be worth it. You'll need about 200g (7oz) fresh or frozen large beans to end up with 100g (3½ oz) here.

Serves 4

8 slices dry-cured streaky bacon
  or 10 slices Parma ham
50g fresh white bread, crusts
  removed, cubed
a knob of unsalted butter
150g (5½oz) mixed red and white
  chicory and rocket
100g (3½oz) cooked French
  beans 100g (3½oz) podded,
  blanched and peeled broad
  beans
5g (⅛oz) fresh flat-leaf parsley,
  picked and washed
extra virgin olive oil
Parmesan shavings (optional)

DRESSING
2 slices white bread, crusts
  removed
4 tbsp milk
juice and finely grated zest of
  1 lemon
2 garlic cloves, peeled
140g (5oz) fresh shelled walnuts
150ml (5fl oz) extra virgin olive oil
salt and freshly ground black
  pepper

1 To make the dressing, tear the bread into the blender and moisten with the milk. Add the lemon zest and juice, garlic and walnuts and blend to a paste. Add, and blend in, the olive oil and some salt and pepper to taste.

2 Grill the bacon or Parma ham until crisp. Fry the cubed bread in a little butter until golden brown.

3 Place the salad leaves and the beans into a bowl. Add the dressing and some salt and pepper and mix.

4 Place a portion of the salad on each plate and top with the crisp bacon, the parsley and croûtons. Drizzle with olive oil and top with the Parmesan shavings.

Lamb, Aubergine and Watercress Salad

A salad in winter? I know what you're thinking, but this one is great: charred aubergine (which we Brits have come to love) served warm with roast loin of lamb. I put watercress and coriander in the salad with red onions, but spring onions will work well, too. The lamb comes from the best end, which has been removed from the bone and trimmed down.

Serves 6

1 x 600g (1lb 5oz) lamb loin,
    trimmed of fat and silver skin
olive oil
salt and freshly ground black
    pepper
2 small aubergines, cut into 1.5cm
    (⅝in) slices

BALSAMIC VINAIGRETTE
4 tbsp balsamic vinegar
1 garlic clove, peeled and finely
    chopped
a pinch of caster sugar
125ml (4fl oz) olive oil
2 fresh thyme sprigs, leaves
    picked and washed

WATERCRESS SALAD
100g (3½oz) watercress, stems
    removed
25g (1oz) fresh coriander, leaves
    picked
1 red chilli, seeded and cut into
    strips
1 red onion, peeled and sliced
rind of ½ salted lemon or
    preserved lemon, cut into strips

1 Preheat the oven to 220°C/425°F/gas mark 7.

2 Brush the lamb with olive oil and season with salt and pepper. Heat a frying pan over a high heat and seal the lamb on all sides until browned. Transfer the lamb to a baking tray and roast for 6-8 minutes for medium. Set aside to rest for 5 minutes before slicing.

3 Preheat an overhead grill or ridged cast-iron grill to a high heat. Lightly brush the aubergine with olive oil and cook for 5-8 minutes, or until tender and browned. Keep warm.

4 Meanwhile, to make the balsamic vinaigrette, whisk all the ingredients together until combined. Season to taste with salt and pepper.

5 To make the salad, combine the watercress, coriander, chilli, onion and lemon rind. Add enough balsamic vinaigrette to moisten it.

6 To serve, place 2-3 slices of aubergine on each serving plate. Slice the lamb loin into discs, about 5mm (¼in) thick, and toss through the salad. Arrange the salad over the aubergine. Finish with a further light drizzle of balsamic vinaigrette.

Baked Crab with a Cheesy Crust

There's a great supplier called Nobles in Whitby. In high season they are knocking out 1,000-plus crabs a day, and not just cooking them but dressing them as well. Their hands are like iron as they rip the shells away while picking the meat out. Crabs are far better than lobsters for flavour and value, and they are much easier to get hold of too.

Serves 4

meat from 4 freshly cooked crabs
25g (1oz) unsalted butter, melted
juice of ½ lemon
1 tsp English mustard
salt and freshly ground black
    pepper
a pinch of medium curry powder
15g (½oz) fresh white
    breadcrumbs
25g (1oz) Parmesan, freshly grated

TO SERVE
1 tbsp balsamic vinegar
3 tbsp extra virgin olive oil
85g (3oz) mixed salad leaves
1 lemon, cut into wedges

1 Preheat the oven to 220°C/425°F/gas mark 7.

2 Mix the brown and white crab-meat in a bowl. Stir in the melted butter, lemon juice and mustard, and season with salt and pepper to taste. Divide this mixture among the crab shells. Place the shells on a baking sheet.

3 Mix the remaining dry ingredients and sprinkle over the crab-meat. Bake until golden, about 6-8 minutes.

4 Combine the vinegar and oil with a little salt and pepper and use this to dress the salad leaves. Serve the crab and salad with lemon wedges.

Drop the live crab into plenty of cold salted water. Bring to the boil.

Simmer for 15 minutes for smaller crabs; 20-25 minutes for larger ones.

Mussel and Saffron Soup with Caramelized Onions and Garlic Croûtons

This cheap soup has great strong flavours, but go carefully; a common mistake is to use too much saffron, as it takes a while to get the right colour and flavour. The soup goes well with the caramelized onions, which I like to make loads of at a time – I also use it on sandwiches and with cheese, especially Cheddar.

Serves 6

50 black mussels, scrubbed and bearded (discard any that do not close when tapped)
75ml (2½fl oz) dry white wine
1 tbsp olive oil
2 tsp minced garlic
a pinch of crushed red pepper flakes
½ small onion, peeled and chopped
1 tsp tomato purée
200ml (7fl oz) double cream, whipped
500ml (18fl oz) fresh chicken stock
1 tsp saffron strands
1 tbsp chopped fresh chives
salt and freshly ground black pepper

CARAMELIZED ONIONS
2 tbsp unsalted butter
2 onions, peeled, halved and thinly sliced

1 Caramelize the onions first. Melt the butter in a medium sauté pan over a low heat. Add the onions and sauté until caramel-brown, about 30 minutes, stirring occasionally.

2 To make the soup, combine the mussels and wine in a large, heavy pot over a high heat. Cover and cook, shaking the pot occasionally, until the mussels open, about 4-5 minutes. Discard any mussels that do not open. Drain, reserving the mussel liquor. Shell 40 of the mussels. Strain the reserved mussel liquor through a fine sieve.

3 In a large saucepan over a medium heat, heat the olive oil, and sauté the garlic and pepper flakes until the garlic is light brown. Add the chopped onion and sauté until tender, about 5 minutes. Add the reserved mussel liquor, the tomato purée, cream and stock. Bring to a boil and skim off any foam that develops.

4 Lower the heat, add the saffron and simmer for 5 minutes. Add the shelled mussels and the chives, and season with salt and pepper. Liquidize.

5 To serve, place a spoonful of caramelized onions in the centre of each bowl and scatter a few mussels around in their shells. Then pour the soup over the lot.

Rich Onion Soup with Cheese Toasts

The start of this recipe is most important. The knack of making a good onion soup is colouring the onions well first, as this will give flavour and a deep colour to the finished dish. No gravy browning – that's cheating!

Serves 6

5 onions, peeled and thinly sliced
3 garlic cloves, peeled and
    thinly sliced
20g (¾oz) duck fat
300ml (10fl oz) red wine
150ml (5fl oz) fresh beef stock
50ml (2fl oz) brandy
100ml (3½fl oz) good balsamic
    vinegar
salt and freshly ground black
    pepper
10g (¼oz) fresh flat-leaf parsley
55g (2oz) unsalted butter

CHEESE TOASTS
8 thick slices white bread
280g (10oz) Gruyère cheese

1 Sauté the onion and garlic in a large pan in the duck fat for about 20-30 minutes, colouring very well.

2 Stir before adding the red wine and stock. Bring to the boil and simmer for about 10 minutes. Add the brandy and balsamic vinegar and simmer for another 20 minutes.

3 Preheat the grill well. Toast the bread on both sides, top with the grated cheese and place under the grill to melt.

4 Season the soup well with salt and pepper and add the chopped fresh parsley. Pour into soup bowls. Top with the grilled cheese toasts and a knob of butter.

Roast Tomato and Cumin Soup

Roasting veg for soups, as I've done here and in the squash soup on page 94, makes the soup taste even better. Remember that it's winter, and English toms aren't around, so this is a good way of bringing flavour to imported ones. Serve with thick slices of crusty bread.

Serves 6-8

1.25kg (2¾lb) ripe tomatoes
6 tbsp olive oil
2 medium onions, peeled and
   roughly chopped
3 garlic cloves, peeled and
   roughly chopped
1 large fresh red chilli pepper,
   chopped
2 tbsp cumin seeds, roasted and
   ground
500ml (18fl oz) tomato passata
salt and freshly ground black
   pepper

1   Preheat the oven to 170°C/325°F/gas mark 3.

2   Slice the tomatoes in half and place them on a large, heavy baking sheet. Sprinkle over 2 tbsp of the olive oil and roast for about 1 hour, or until the tomatoes are dehydrated and have caramelized. Remove the tomatoes from the baking sheet and set aside.

3   Place the onion, garlic and chilli in a large saucepan with the remaining olive oil. Cook over a low heat, stirring occasionally, until the onion is soft and translucent, about 10 minutes. Add the cumin and fry for another 5 minutes. Add the roasted tomatoes and the tomato passata and cook for 10 minutes.

4   Purée the mixture in a food processor or blender.

5   To serve, transfer the mixture back into a saucepan and reheat gently until warm. Taste and add salt and pepper as desired. Ladle into warm bowls. Serve with some charred ciabatta.

Pea Soup

I was brought up on this, and I love it! My gran used to put chunks of leftover ham with the bone in this soup, which adds extra flavour. I like it with fresh mint leaves thrown in at the end. But soups can be easily overcooked and none more so than this: the last thing you want is a wrinkly bullet in the bottom of your soup bowl.

Serves 6-8

1 bunch spring or young green-
stemmed onions, chopped
2 garlic cloves, peeled and chopped
25g (1oz) unsalted butter
600g (1lb 5oz) podded young peas
675g (1½lb) leftover cooked/
boiled ham, roughly chopped
600ml (1 pint) fresh chicken stock
250ml (9fl oz) double cream
(optional)
salt and ground black pepper
1 mint sprig (8-12 leaves), chopped

1   Sweat the onion and garlic in the butter in a covered pan for 5 minutes, without colouring.

2   Add the peas, ham and stock, and bring to the boil. If using the cream, add now and simmer until the peas are tender, about 10 minutes.

3   Season to taste, and liquidize if you like, adding another 25g (1oz) butter. But why bother blending? I think it looks and tastes so much better when you can see the bits of food you're eating (and without the extra cream). Serve sprinkled with the mint.

Sweetcorn and Crab Soup

This may be taking its place in a British cookbook, but the idea came from one of the Indian chefs in my restaurant. Yuri makes great soup, and this is one of my favourites.

Serves 6

1 large white onion, peeled
250g (9oz) potatoes, peeled
curry powder
30g (1¼oz) unsalted butter
1.2 litres (2 pints) chicken stock
handful of fresh basil leaves
300ml (10fl oz) double cream
450g (1lb) frozen sweetcorn
kernels
meat from 2 freshly cooked crabs
olive oil

1   Dice the onion and potatoes. In a large, heavy pan, sweat them with curry powder to taste in the butter until soft. Pour in the stock, stir, and bring to the boil, then simmer until the potato is tender, about 15 minutes.

2   Meanwhile, whizz most of the basil in a blender until finely chopped. Add 250ml (9fl oz) of the double cream and mix. Season and chill.

3   Add the sweetcorn to the soup, simmer for 3 minutes, then add the crabmeat and remove from the heat. Purée while still hot, then return to the pan, add the remaining cream, and simmer for 3 minutes. Season. Spoon into bowls. Add a little basil cream and olive oil and a basil leaf.

Smoked Haddock Risotto with Saffron, Peas and Grilled Fennel

I love to give an unusual twist to a great British classic – and here's my version of that Brit favourite, smoked haddock soup. It's ideal for those cool days when autumn is turning into winter and fennel is in season.

**Serves 4 as a main,
8 as a starter**

750g (1lb 10oz) undyed smoked
 haddock
about 1.2 litres (40fl oz) fresh fish
 or vegetable stock
2 fennel bulbs, trimmed and sliced
1 small white onion, peeled and
 sliced
85g (3oz) unsalted butter
450g (1lb) arborio rice
100ml (3½fl oz) white wine
a pinch of saffron strands
140g (5oz) Parmesan, grated
175g (6oz) frozen peas
10g (¼oz) mixed fresh parsley
 and coriander leaves
85g (3oz) mascarpone cheese
salt and freshly ground black
 pepper
1 lemon, cut into wedges

1 Skin the haddock and pick over to remove any bones. Cut the fish into dice. Heat the stock on top of the stove.

2 Put half of the fennel slices and all the onion slices in a suitable pan with the butter and cook for about 3 minutes. Add the rice and cook for a further minute. Add the wine and saffron and stir until the wine has been absorbed.

3 Gradually add ladlefuls of the hot stock, stirring, and waiting until the stock has been absorbed by the rice before adding any more. After about 10 minutes, add the diced haddock and continue to cook until the rice is tender, about another 5 minutes.

4 Meanwhile, grill the remaining fennel slices until tender and golden, about 3-4 minutes.

5 Add the Parmesan, peas, herbs and mascarpone to the risotto and stir to heat the peas through. Season to taste. Serve the risotto with the grilled fennel on top, and a wedge of lemon to the side.

Thai Chicken Cakes with Sweet Chilli Sauce

I know these little cakes aren't classically British, but we love them don't we? They make a great starter or snack. If you want to cool the sauce down for the kids, mix it with a little crème fraîche. You can also place the chicken mixture on skewers – it looks great.

.

Serves 4 as a starter

2 chicken breasts, skinned and
  cubed
1 garlic clove, peeled and roughly
  chopped
1 x 1cm ($\frac{1}{2}$in) knob fresh root
  ginger, peeled and chopped
1 small onion, peeled and roughly
  chopped
2 tbsp chopped fresh coriander
1 green chilli, roughly chopped
salt and freshly ground black
  pepper
2 tbsp olive oil

CHILLI SAUCE
55g (2oz) caster sugar
2 red chillies, chopped
1 tomato, chopped
4 Kaffir lime leaves
2 lemongrass stalks, finely
  chopped
25g (1oz) fresh root ginger, peeled
  and chopped
2 garlic cloves, peeled and
  chopped
1 shallot, peeled and chopped
2 tbsp fish sauce
25ml (1fl oz) sesame oil
50ml (2fl oz) dark soy sauce
2 tbsp clear honey
juice and finely grated zest of
  2 limes

TO SERVE
4 spring onions, trimmed and
  finely sliced

1 To make the chilli sauce place the sugar in a pan on a medium heat and heat gently to a caramel colour. Don't let it burn.

2 Meanwhile, purée all the rest of the sauce ingredients in a blender. Pour into the caramel-coloured sugar and stir well. Bring to the boil and cook for about 5 minutes, simmering gently. Allow to cool, season with salt and pepper and chill in the fridge.

3 Place the chicken, garlic, ginger, onion, coriander and chilli in a food processor and season to taste with salt and pepper. Blitz for 15-20 seconds. Shape the chicken mixture into small cakes.

4 Heat the olive oil in a frying pan over a moderate heat and fry the chicken cakes until golden on both sides and cooked through, about 3-4 minutes in total.

5 Serve immediately, with the sweet chilli sauce and spring onions.

MEAT AND GAME BIRDS

We Brits produce some really great meat, so why mess about with it? Simple terrines and great roasts with all the trimmings helped to build our nation! I really believe in using the whole animal; I used to love watching my grandad carefully fry calves' liver.

Fillet of Beef with Prune and Potato Cakes

For my college exam in the early 1990s, I had to make a classic potato dish call Pommes Anna, which is a layered cake of potatoes and butter cooked in a mould. It's a pain in the backside to make and was a pretty pointless exercise as I've never made it since. However, people love rösti, which is made with grated spuds, and this is a mixture of the two.

Serves 4

4 x 200g (7oz) fillet steaks
25g (1oz) unsalted butter
extra virgin olive oil
1 small white onion, peeled
  and diced
2 garlic cloves, peeled
  and chopped
200g (7oz) fresh chanterelle
  mushrooms, washed and dried
2 tomatoes, diced
5g (⅛oz) fresh parsley leaves,
  chopped
salt and freshly ground black
  pepper
85g (3 oz) washed and destemmed
  spinach leaves

RED WINE SAUCE
½ red onion, peeled and chopped
2 tbsp extra virgin olive oil
750ml (1 pint 7fl oz) fresh beef
  stock
⅓ bottle red wine
10g (¼oz) unsalted butter

PRUNE AND POTATO CAKE
450g (1lb) baking potatoes
100g (3½oz) unsalted butter,
  melted
8 fresh prunes, stoned and
  chopped

1 Preheat the oven to 200°C/400°F/gas mark 6. To make the red wine sauce, sauté the onion in the oil until it has softened, about 2 minutes, then add the stock and red wine. Bring to the boil, then simmer to reduce to a good sauce consistency. Pass through a sieve, add the butter, and keep warm to one side.

2 For the potato cakes, peel and sculpt the potatoes into barrel shapes. Slice very thinly on a mandolin. Mix the slices with the melted butter and season with salt and pepper.

3 Using 4 holes of a 6-hole Yorkshire pudding tin, or 4 x 7.5cm (3in) non-stick tins, layer the potato, about 4 slices thick, and then add a few chopped prunes. Top with the same amount of potatoes again. Don't worry if the potato is higher than the tins; it will collapse while cooking. Bake for 30 minutes, then remove from the oven and allow to cool. Remove from the tins and keep to one side, leaving the oven on.

4 Meanwhile, cook the fillets. Heat up a shallow frying pan on the stove and place the seasoned fillets in the dry pan. Colour well on one side before turning over and adding half the butter and the same amount of olive oil.

5 In a separate pan, sauté the onion, garlic and chanterelles in the remaining butter, then add 200ml (7fl oz) of the red wine sauce (if you have any left over, reserve it for use another time), the tomatoes and chopped parsley. Season to taste.

6 To serve, wilt the spinach in a pan with just the water clinging to the leaves. Drain the spinach well, then place on the plates, top with a potato cake and then a steak. Finish by spooning the sauce and mushrooms over the top.

Peppered Roast Beef

Do I have to say anything? Just look at it and eat it! The Yorkshire has loads of eggs in it, but it works – *if* you place the mix in hot tins, *if* you leave the oven door closed and *if* you make the mixture in advance and leave it to rest. This is the best recipe for Yorkies I've ever tasted. If I can't make Yorkshire pud coming from where I do, then I should shoot myself!

Serves 8

1 x 6-rib joint of beef
salt and freshly ground black
   pepper
cooking fat or oil
1 large fresh rosemary sprig,
   leaves picked

1 Preheat the oven to 220°C/425°F/gas mark 7. Season the beef with plenty of pepper and a sprinkle of salt.

2 Heat some oil or fat in a hot roasting pan, then add the meat to seal. Remove from the heat, sprinkle with rosemary leaves, and place in the oven. A joint of this size will take 1½-2 hours to cook, but this depends on how you like to eat it. Cooking for 1 hour will keep it rare; 2 hours, medium; 2½ hours, medium-to-well-done.

3 Once cooked, leave the meat to rest for 15-20 minutes before carving. This will relax the meat, and it will become even more tender. Serve with Yorkshire pudding (below), roast potatoes and perhaps parsnips (*see* page 131) and gravy.

Yorkshire Pudding

Serves 4

225g (8oz) plain flour
salt and freshly ground black
   pepper
8 medium free-range eggs
600ml (1 pint) milk
55g (2oz) good dripping or 50ml
   (2fl oz) vegetable oil

1 Place the flour and some seasoning in a bowl and make a well in the middle. Add the eggs one by one, using a whisk, then whisk in the milk, mixing very well until the batter is smooth and there are no lumps. Leave in the fridge for at least an hour or, even better, overnight. Preheat the oven to about 220°C/425°F/gas mark 7.

2 Divide the dripping or oil among 8 Yorkshire pudding tins (13cm/5in in diameter) or 12 muffin tins, and place in the oven to get very hot.

3 Carefully remove the trays from the oven and, with a ladle or a jug, fill the tins with the batter and place back in the oven immediately. Cook for about 20 minutes before opening the door to check – otherwise they will collapse. If undercooked, reduce the heat to 200°C/400°F/gas mark 6 and cook for a further 10-15 minutes. Serve immediately

Pork Terrine with Apricots and Pistachios

Good sausages are used as the base of this simple terrine. You could play around with the flavours by using beef or game sausages instead of pork. I've used plum sauce, as this combines with the orange segments to give a sweet-and-sour flavour. When making terrines, make sure you don't overcook them or they will break up while being sliced.

Serves 8-12

olive oil
250g (9oz) streaky bacon rashers
900g (2lb) or 14-15 large sausages
  (Lincolnshire are best)
10 fresh sage leaves, chopped
5g ($^1/_8$oz) fresh flat-leaf parsley,
  chopped
100g (3$^1/_2$oz) dried apricots,
  chopped
75g (2$^3/_4$oz) shelled pistachio
  nuts, roughly chopped
salt and freshly ground black
  pepper

SALAD
2 oranges, peeled and segmented
55g (2oz) wild rocket leaves
1 large potato, peeled, cooked
  and diced
8 tbsp plum sauce (make your
  own, or buy the Chinese stuff
  from the supermarket)
3 tbsp olive oil

1   Preheat the oven to 180°C/350°F/gas mark 4. Take a terrine dish, 30-35cm (12-14in) long, 10cm (4in) wide, and 9-10cm (3 $^1/_2$-4in) deep, and brush it with olive oil. Line the dish with streaky bacon, leaving 5-6cm (2-2$^1/_2$in) overlapping the edge of the terrine.

2   Make the filling by removing all the meat from the sausage skins (discard these). Add the sage, parsley, chopped apricots and pistachio nuts and mix well with plenty of seasoning.

3   Pile the meat mixture into the terrine mould and press down well. Fold over the bacon and either cover with the lid or with foil, and place in a bain-marie half-filled with hot water. Cook in the oven for 60 minutes. Remove from the oven, cover with foil, and press down with a weight. Cool, then place in the fridge.

4   When ready to serve, make the salad by mixing the orange segments, rocket and potato together in a bowl. Mix the plum sauce with the olive oil and seasoning to taste.

5   Cut the terrine into slices and serve in the centre of the plates with the salad around and the dressing spooned over the top.

Yorkshire Ham Terrine with Spiced Pickle

Scotts butchers in York is still the best place to buy Yorkshire gammon and ham, but if you visit you have to queue. Last time I was there it was obviously pension day, as the place was like a gala bingo hall on a jackpot night.

Serves 10

3 ham knuckles
4 bay leaves
6 black peppercorns
1 large onion, peeled and halved
1 medium leek, halved
1 medium carrot, peeled and halved
extra virgin olive oil
6-8 thin slices York ham, or other cooked sliced ham
2 shallots, peeled and finely chopped
1 garlic clove, peeled
salt and freshly ground black pepper
20g (¾oz) fresh parsley leaves, finely chopped
a pinch of ground mixed spice
2 gelatine leaves, soaked in cold water for 5 minutes
55g (2oz) mixed salad leaves and herbs (chervil, wild rocket, etc)

PINEAPPLE PICKLE
1 garlic clove, peeled and crushed
1 tsp grain mustard
5 tbsp white wine vinegar
a good pinch of turmeric powder
150g (5½oz) demerara sugar
1 medium pineapple, skinned, cored and finely chopped

DRESSING
4 tbsp each of grain mustard, extra virgin olive oil and cider vinegar

1 Put the ham knuckles, bay leaves, peppercorns, onion, leek and carrot in a large saucepan. Cover with cold water, bring to the boil and simmer, covered, for 3 hours, until the meat is tender.

2 Meanwhile, grease a 20 x 8cm (8 x 3 ¼in) terrine mould with olive oil. Line with clingfilm, then with the sliced York ham.

3 When the ham knuckles are nearly cooked, heat a little olive oil in a small pan and gently sweat the shallots and whole garlic clove.

4 Remove the cooked ham knuckles from the pan, reserving the stock, and leave to cool slightly. While warm, remove the meat in pieces from the bone. Place in a small bowl with the shallot and garlic, some salt and pepper and the parsley. Mix well, then pack into the terrine mould.

5 Strain the ham stock. Taste and, if it is too salty, dilute with water. Pour 500ml (18fl oz) into a pan and add the mixed spice. Warm gently and add the soaked gelatine; leave for 2-3 minutes for the gelatine to dissolve before stirring. Pour into the terrine and overlap the edges of the ham. Cover with clingfilm; the terrine needs to be quite solid and "packed". Put a uniform weight on the terrine to press it down (I use a brick) and leave overnight in the fridge.

6 To make the pickle, put all the ingredients together in a pan except for the pineapple. Simmer for 3 minutes, then add the pineapple and cook for a further 3 minutes. Put into sterilized jars and cool.

7 To make the mustard seed dressing, whisk all the ingredients together, then use some of it to dress the salad leaves at the last minute.

8 To serve, turn out the terrine and remove the clingfilm. Using a sharp knife, cut into 2cm (¾in) slices and place a slice in the centre of each plate. On each plate, spoon a pile of pineapple pickle, placing a few dressed leaves on, too. Grind over a little black pepper, and serve.

Pot-roast Pheasant with Cider and Calvados

While doing the photography for this book I went shooting at Jody Schekter's farm up the road from me. It was a great day and, as usual, the number of birds we said we shot was different to the number we took home. Typical men, I know! If you buy a brace of birds, or a cock and a hen, remember hens are smaller so will need to be removed before the cocks.

Serves 4

55g (2oz) butter
2 pheasants, cleaned
salt and freshly ground black
    pepper
1 onion, finely chopped
85g (3oz) bacon lardons
1 stick celery, chopped
1 carrot, peeled and chopped
4 sprigs sage
2 Granny Smith apples, peeled,
    cored and cut into large chunks
50ml (2fl oz) calvados
500ml (18fl oz) dry cider
290ml (½ pint) chicken stock
290ml (½ pint) double cream

BAKED APPLES

4 Cox's apples, peeled and cored
25g (1oz) melted butter
1 tbsp soft light brown sugar

TO SERVE

deep-fried sage leaves
8 slices of crispy cooked pancetta
kale, blanched

1   Preheat oven to 190°C/375°F/gas mark 5. Melt the butter in a large non-stick casserole pot. Season the pheasants with salt and ground black pepper. Place the pheasants into the casserole pot and brown until pale golden on all sides. Remove from the pot and set aside.

2   Add the onion, bacon, celery, carrot and sage sprigs to the pot and cook over a medium heat until the onion is soft and translucent and the bacon is crispy. Carefully pour off any excess fat from the lardons.

3   Return the pheasants to the pot and scatter over the apples. Pour over most of the calvados and set alight. Once the flames have died down, add 290ml (½ pint) of the cider and the chicken stock. Bring to a gentle simmer, cover and place in the oven for about 20 minutes, until the birds are cooked through.

4   For the baked apples, place the apples on a baking tray that has been brushed with a little butter and sprinkle with the sugar. Bake for about ½ hour, basting the apples a few times during cooking.

5   Remove the pheasants from the pot and place on a chopping board. Remove the thighs and breasts and set aside to keep warm. Chop the carcass into 4 pieces and place them back in the pot with the vegetables with the remaining cider. Bring to a boil and simmer gently for 5 minutes.

6   Strain the sauce into a bowl through a fine-meshed sieve. Pour the strained sauce back into the pot and add a splash of calvados. Reduce by half. Add the cream and simmer for a further 5 minutes, or until the sauce is creamy and slightly thickened. Return the pheasant breasts and thighs to the pot to warm through and become coated in the sauce.

7   Remove the baked apples from the oven. Serve the pheasant on a bed of kale with a baked apple. Garnish with deep-fried sage leaves and crispy pancetta.

Honey-roast Duck Confit with Tomato Beans

I made this dish up while doing a dinner party in Scotland, and it's now a favourite. Canned beans and canned tomatoes can taste great heated together as we all know – think of beans on toast – but this goes to another level.

Serves 4

4 duck legs
fine salt and freshly ground black
    pepper
2-3 fresh thyme sprigs, leaves
    picked off
300g (10½oz) duck fat
2 tbsp clear honey

TOMATO BEANS
4 tbsp extra virgin olive oil
1 white onion, peeled and
    finely chopped
4 garlic cloves, peeled and
    finely chopped
100ml (3 ½fl oz) white wine
2 fresh thyme sprigs
1 x 400g can chopped tomatoes
6 medium tomatoes
1 x 350g can flageolet beans,
    drained and rinsed
55g (2oz) unsalted butter
10g (¼oz) fresh parsley, chopped

RED WINE SAUCE
½ red onion, peeled and chopped
2 tbsp extra virgin olive oil
750ml (1 pint 7fl oz) fresh beef
    stock
⅓ bottle red wine
10g (¼oz) unsalted butter

1   To make the duck confit, weigh the legs, then put them on a small tray. Sprinkle with 15g (½oz) salt per kg, and the fresh thyme leaves. Cover with clingfilm and place in the fridge overnight.

2   Remove the legs from the tray, wipe off the salt, and put them in a frying pan with the duck fat. Cook slowly, covered, for about 2½ hours, turning occasionally. Leave to cool in the fat.

3   When you are about half an hour from serving, preheat the oven to 180°C/350°F/gas mark 4.

4   To make the beans, heat the olive oil in a pan and sauté the onion and garlic for a few minutes. Add the wine, thyme and tomatoes, both canned and fresh, and bring to a simmer. After 15 minutes, add the beans and simmer for a further 15 minutes. Season with salt and pepper, and add the butter and parsley to finish. Keep warm.

5   To make the red wine sauce, sauté the onion in the oil until it is softened, about 2 minutes, then add the stock and red wine. Bring to the boil, then simmer to reduce to a good sauce consistency. Pass through a sieve, add the butter, and keep warm to one side.

6   Meanwhile, scrape the fat from the duck legs and place in a roasting pan. Smear the honey over the duck legs, then roast for 20 minutes, spooning the honey glaze over the legs at least a couple of times, until cooked through.

7   To serve, place the beans on the plates and top with the duck confit. Spoon the sauce around.

Duck Liver Pâté with Pear Chutney

I hated liver as a kid, as most kids do. The only two dishes my grandad would cook were calves' liver and poached haddock. I used to watch him with his Brylcreemed stick-back hair as he pan-fried his slice of liver with precision. He never failed to try to get me to eat some as I ran out of the door in horror. I now know I was missing out on something great.

Serves 14-16

1kg (2¼lb) organic duck livers, left whole, but all green and thready bits removed
Cognac
2 garlic cloves, peeled and finely chopped
a handful of fresh basil leaves
salt and freshly ground black pepper
350g (12oz) unsalted butter

GARNISH
brown bread, sliced and toasted, or Melba toast
pear chutney
mixed salad leaves, dressed

1   Place the livers in a single layer in a heatproof dish, and scatter over some Cognac. It should not cover them, but they need to wallow in it for several hours. Turn them over so both sides absorb the alcohol. The garlic, all but 2 of the basil leaves (torn and minus the stalks) and some salt and pepper should be thrown into the brew just before poaching.

2   Gently poach the livers, turning them over after a couple of minutes, and continue to stew until they are cooked on the outside but pink within, about 3-4 minutes, until cooked. Do not overcook or you will end up with a drab, brown, crumbly result.

3   Tip the contents of the dish straight into your blender with 225g (8oz) of the softened butter, and whiz until smooth. Check the seasoning, then scrape into a large terrine dish and leave to cool.

4   Meanwhile, clarify the remaining butter. Gently melt it, and pour into another container, leaving behind all the curd-like sediment. Cool a little.

5   Pour the buttercup-coloured clear liquid butter over the surface of the pâté, place the reserved basil leaves in the centre, and put it into the fridge until set.

6   Using a hot knife, slice the terrine. Serve with a slice of toast, a spoonful of chutney and some dressed mixed salad leaves.

VEGETABLES

We have so many fantastic winter veg! Our roots are brilliant, yet we seem to forget about so many of them. Beetroot is a particular favourite of mine, yet loads of people I know don't like it. I reckon if they tried it well cooked they'd quickly change their minds. I recommend growing your own veg – I've just planted my own veg patch in my garden and I can't wait until the new season to try it!

Red Onion and Crème Fraîche Tarts

I use red onions for this instead of Spanish white onions because they require much less cooking and because they start off red, but instantly turn a dark, deep, rich caramel when you add balsamic. I serve this in my restaurant on the ship, and it always proves popular. I've just planted red onions in my garden and am looking forward to the new season.

Serves 4

250g (9oz) ready-rolled puff pastry (defrosted if frozen)
1 small egg, beaten
salt and freshly ground black pepper
100ml (3½fl oz) olive oil, plus extra for drizzling
2 tbsp balsamic vinegar
100g (3½oz) fresh rocket leaves

Filling

3 large red onions, peeled and thinly sliced
6 garlic cloves, peeled and crushed
4 fresh thyme sprigs
25g (1oz) unsalted butter
125g (4½oz) full-fat crème fraîche

1   If using frozen pastry, allow it to defrost. Preheat the oven to 220°C/425°F/gas mark 7. Roll the puff pastry out until it is half as thick as it was when it was opened (about 3mm thick, or as thin as you dare) and cut into 4 round circles the size of a side plate. Using a sharp knife, cut a small, frame-like edge around the whole pastry and lay this, in pieces, around the outer edge of the tarts. Alternatively, make 1 large rectangular tart.

2   Break the egg into a bowl and whisk with a fork. Brush the pastry circles or rectangle around the edges. Dock with a fork before baking for 15-20 minutes, until the pastry is cooked.

3   For the filling, in a large pan fry the onions, garlic and thyme in the butter for 15 minutes, until well caramelized. Season well. Remove the cooked base/s from the oven and spread with the crème fraiche, then top with the caramelized onions, drizzle with olive oil and return to the oven for a few minutes, until cooked.

4   In a bowl, mix the balsamic vinegar with the olive oil and some salt and pepper. Combine the salad leaves with the dressing.

5   Remove the tart/s from the oven and place on a serving plate. Drizzle with a little olive oil and serve with a small pile of the dressed salad in the middle of the tart.

Beetroot and Mascarpone Risotto

A not-so-British dish, but we've come to love risotto and this dish uses my favourite British winter veg – beetroot! Served with salmon and cauliflower in a salad, or simply cooked in a risotto like this, it gives fantastic flavour and is a good way of introducing beetroot to those who think they don't like it. A mate of mine loves this risotto with a seared steak and salad.

Serves 4

6 raw beetroots, peeled and
 roughly chopped
500ml (18fl oz) fresh vegetable
 stock
2 garlic cloves, peeled and finely
 chopped
2 shallots, peeled and finely
 chopped
2 fresh thyme sprigs
25g (1oz) unsalted butter
225g (8oz) arborio rice
100ml (3½fl oz) white wine
3 tbsp mascarpone cheese
2 tbsp chopped fresh parsley
115g (4oz) Parmesan, freshly
 grated
salt and freshly ground black
 pepper

1 Blend the beetroot in the food processor with half the stock and leave it to one side. Have the remaining stock warming in a pan on the stove.

2 Put the garlic, shallot and thyme in a pan in the butter and sweat for about a minute. Add the rice and stir to coat with the butter. Add the wine and cook, stirring, until it evaporates.

3 Add a ladleful of beetroot stock and, stirring continuously, bring to the boil. Once this has been absorbed by the rice, add another ladleful and bring to the boil again. Keep going like this until all the beetroot stock is used up. Then continue the process with the hot vegetable stock. Simmer for about 12 minutes in all, stirring, until the rice is cooked but still has a little bite.

4 Once the rice is cooked, stir in the mascarpone, parsley, Parmesan and salt and pepper. Serve hot.

Salad of Chargrilled Leeks and Red Onions with Mozzarella

The thing I love most about this dish is the dressing; I sometimes serve it with plain little gem lettuce and some croûtons or, even better, warm French beans and seared tuna or salmon. You can change this salad totally by adding smoked chicken or plainly cooked chicken. You don't have to use mozzarella, but you should choose a mild cheese.

Serves 4

a pinch of caster sugar
salt and freshly ground black
    pepper
24 young leeks, trimmed
2 red onions, peeled and cut into
    wedges
2 x 200g mozzarella balls, cut into
    4 slices each

DRESSING
4 tbsp tarragon vinegar
1 tsp Dijon mustard
1 tbsp chopped fresh tarragon
50ml (2fl oz) extra virgin olive oil
1 tomato, seeded and finely diced
1 tbsp fine capers, rinsed and
    drained
1 tbsp stoned green olives, finely
    chopped
1 hard-boiled egg, shelled and
    finely chopped

1 Make the dressing first. Combine all the ingredients and leave for an hour or so for the flavours to come together.

2 Bring a large pan of water to the boil with the sugar and a little salt. Throw in the leeks, return to the boil and cook gently for 2-3 minutes. Drain them well and dry on a cloth.

3 Grill the leeks and onions on a hot, ridged cast-iron griddle pan. When they are tender and slightly blackened, remove from the heat and season with salt and pepper.

4 Toss the leeks and onions in the dressing, then divide among 4 plates. Arrange 2 slices of mozzarella over each portion, and serve.

Roasted Vegetables with Rosemary and Honey

This is a fab way to serve veg if you are doing a dinner party or a Sunday lunch. It's a bucket-load less stressful than five pans of boiling water with overcooked roots inside! Just chop everything up, sprinkle and drizzle, and throw it in the oven.

Serves 6

450g (1lb) new potatoes
450g (1lb) parsnips
450g (1lb) carrots
225g (8oz) fennel bulbs
225g (8oz) red onions
6 tbsp olive oil
75ml (2½fl oz) clear honey
25g (1oz) unsalted butter
1 fresh rosemary sprig, torn into
    4 pieces
salt and freshly ground black
    pepper
1 lemon (optional)

1 Preheat the oven to 220°C/425°F/gas mark 7.

2 Wash the potatoes, parsnips, carrots and fennel, but don't peel them, then slice into large chunky pieces. Cut the red onions into quarters.

3 Place all the vegetables into an oven tray and drizzle with olive oil and honey. Add the butter in knobs and sprinkle on the rosemary. Season well. Roast for 30-40 minutes.

4 Remove from the oven and coat all the vegetables in the glaze in the base of the pan. Serve with some lemon juice squeezed over if you like.

Shallot Tarte Tatin

I love to make classic dishes easy – and this one really is simple. Tarte tatin is French, but over the years we've nicked it, and now it's ours, too!

Serves 4

350g (12oz) shallots, peeled
olive oil
115g (4oz) caster sugar
25g (1oz) unsalted butter
salt and freshly ground black
   pepper
200g (7oz) ready-rolled puff pastry

TO SERVE
225g (8oz) goat's cheese
8 tbsp runny honey
truffle oil
30g (1¼oz) wild rocket leaves

1 Preheat the oven to 200°C/400°F/gas mark 6.

2 Roast the shallots with a little olive oil for 20 minutes.

3 In a clean non-stick ovenproof pan, melt the sugar to a caramel. Add the butter and mix with the caramel. While hot, pour the mixture into 4 x 7.5cm (3in) non-stick Yorkshire pudding tins. Add the roasted shallots until each tin is full and a tight fit. Season with salt and pepper.

4 Cut the puff pastry into 4 circles about 1cm (½in) bigger than the tins. Place the pastry on top of the shallots, and tuck in the edges down the side of the tins to seal in the shallots. Place the tins in the oven and bake for 15 minutes, until the pastry is cooked.

5 Meanwhile, preheat the grill to medium. With a sharp knife, cut the goat's cheese in 1cm (½in) slices.

6 Turn the tarts out, while piping hot, on to an oven tray. Top with slices of goat's cheese and place under the grill for a few minutes to brown the cheese.

7 Meanwhile, mix the honey and a little truffle oil together. Place a tart on each plate and garnish with the rocket dressed with the honey and truffle oil.

Quick Onion Bhajis

This recipe isn't really mine, as it comes from one of my boys in the bistro kitchen. I promised him I'd put them in the book. I hope you like these as much as I do. I know bhajis are not really British, but we've kind of adopted them. To make a good dip for them, mix some ground cumin, lime juice and chopped mint into some Greek yoghurt.

Makes 8-10

2 onions, peeled and thinly sliced
70g (2½oz) self-raising flour
1 tsp medium curry powder
½ tsp ground cumin
2 tsp turmeric powder
½ tsp salt
150ml (5fl oz) plain yoghurt
vegetable oil for deep-frying

1 Place the onions, flour, spices and salt in a bowl and then stir in the plain yoghurt.

2 Divide the mixture into small balls in the palm of your hands.

3 Heat the oil to 180°C/350°F, then deep-fry the bhajis for 1-2 minutes, to colour and cook. Drain on kitchen paper and cool for a while.

4 Serve as required, with either a spiced yoghurt dip (*see* above) or some mango chutney.

Dauphinoise in a Pan

To my mind this is still the best potato dish you can serve in winter. Yes, it's French, and purists will complain that traditionally it's cooked in layers raw in the oven, and not with the cheese. But I'm all for making life easier, and this recipe takes a quarter of the time to cook. When working in France at a three-star Michelin restaurant, this is all I was allowed to eat.

Serves 6

900g (2lb) King Edward potatoes
25g (1oz) unsalted butter
2 garlic cloves, peeled and
    chopped
2 shallots, peeled and chopped
150ml (5fl oz) milk
600ml (1 pint) double cream
salt and freshly ground black
    pepper
55g (2oz) Cheddar, grated
100g (3½oz) mozzarella,
    crumbled
salt and freshly ground black
    pepper

1   Peel and slice the potatoes as thinly as possible (preferably using a mandolin). Melt the butter in a medium heatproof dish or in a large pan, and sauté the garlic and shallot lightly. Add the milk and cream and bring to a simmer. Add the sliced potato, and cook on a gentle simmer for about 8-10 minutes to just cook the potato.

2   Preheat the grill to medium-hot.

3   Season the potatoes well, and either leave in the dish to serve or ladle carefully from the pan into 6 small heatproof dishes. Top with the cheeses, spreading them evenly. Place under the grill for a couple of minutes until brown, then serve.

PUDS

Puds are my thing! Sponge puds, fruit puds, pancakes, ice-creams… they all taste fantastic to me. Of course, we shouldn't be eating heavy puddings every day of the week. But there really can't be any harm in treating ourselves and our families every once in a while, can there? Remember how good classics like Queen of Puds tasted when we were kids? Well, they taste just as good now!

White Chocolate and Raspberry Trifle

This can also be made as individual trifles.

Serves 4

175g (6oz) white chocolate
2 medium egg yolks
25g (1oz) caster sugar
300ml (10fl oz) milk
700ml (1¼ pints) double cream
8 x 4cm (1½in) slices Swiss roll
 (bought or home-made)
2 tbsp kirsch
600g (1lb 5oz) raspberries
a few fresh mint sprigs

1 Put a 55g (2oz) piece of white chocolate in the fridge – this will make it easier to grate later. Break the remainder into small pieces.

2 Cream the egg yolks and caster sugar together in a large bowl. Whisk for about 2-3 minutes, until the mixture is pale, thick and creamy and leaves a trail.

3 Pour the milk and 175ml (6fl oz) of the cream into a small, heavy-based saucepan and bring to the boil. Pour this on to the egg mixture, whisking all the time, then pour it back into the pan and place over a moderate heat. Stir the mixture with a wooden spoon until it starts to thicken and coats the back of the spoon. Add the broken-up pieces of chocolate and stir in until completely incorporated. Remove the pan from the heat and allow to cool slightly. Cover the custard with clingfilm to stop a skin forming.

4 Place half the Swiss roll slices in a large glass bowl and sprinkle with half the kirsch. Scatter over a third of the raspberries, then repeat. Pour the white chocolate custard over the top and leave to set in the fridge.

5 To serve, whip the remaining double cream. Top the custard with a the whipped cream, scatter over the remaining raspberries, grate over the chilled white chocolate and place the mint sprigs on top.

Syrup Sponge with Crushed Raspberries

This sponge pudding should be made in a microwave, as it doesn't steam successfully. It'll take you no longer than 10 minutes.

Serves 4

150g (5½oz) plain flour
1 tsp baking powder
125g (4½oz) unsalted butter, melted
125g (4½oz) caster sugar
2 medium eggs
juice and finely grated zest of 2 small lemons
25ml (1fl oz) milk
vegetable oil, for greasing
4 tbsp golden syrup, or jam if preferred
100g (3½oz) raspberries (fresh if possible, but home-frozen would do)

1   Sift the flour and baking powder together into a bowl. Tip the butter, sugar, eggs, flour and baking powder into a food processor and mix to a paste. Add the lemon juice and zest and continue to mix, adding the milk, until the mixture reaches a dropping consistency.

2   Grease a 1.2-litre (40fl oz) basin suitable for the microwave with a little vegetable oil. Pour in a little of the syrup and all the raspberries. Spoon in the sponge mixture, cover with clingfilm and microwave on full power for 4 minutes (or until the sponge begins to shrink from the side and is springy to the touch).

3   Leave to stand for 2-3 minutes before turning out. Serve with the remaining syrup or jam, and with some "proper" custard if you like (*see* page 70).

Sussex Pond Pudding

This is the best dessert ever, but be warned that it takes a while to make. This is not a dish ever likely to appear at a Weight Watchers' convention dinner, as the amount of butter and sugar is frightening! But you'll forget all about that when you pour double cream over it and have a spoon in your hand…

Serves 4-6

225g (8oz) self-raising flour
115g (4oz) shredded beef suet
75ml (2½fl oz) milk
200g (7oz) slightly salted butter, diced
200g (7oz) soft light brown or caster sugar
2 large lemons

1 Mix the flour and suet together in a bowl. Combine the milk with 75ml (2½fl oz) water in a jug. Mix enough of the wet ingredients into the dry ingredients to make a dough that is soft, but not too soft to roll. Roll this dough out into a large circle, then cut out a quarter of the circle to be used later as the lid of the pudding.

2 Butter a 1.5 litre (2¾ pint) pudding basin lavishly. Drop the three-quarter circle of pastry into it and press the cut sides together to make a perfect join.

3 Put 100g (3½oz) each of the butter and sugar into the pastry-lined basin. Prick the lemons all over with a larding needle so the juices can escape, then put them on to the butter and sugar. Fill the rest of the cavity with the remaining butter and sugar, adding more if you wish to.

4 Lay the reserved pastry on top of the filling and press the edges together so the pudding is sealed in. Put a piece of foil right over the basin with a pleat in the middle. Tie it in place with string and make a string handle over the top so the pudding can be lifted out easily.

5 Put a large pan of water on to boil and lower the pudding into it. The water must be boiling, and it should come halfway, or a little further, up the sides of the basin. Cover and leave to boil for 3-4 hours. If the water gets low, replenish it with boiling water.

6 To serve, remove the basin from the pan and take off the foil lid. Put a deep dish over the basin and quickly turn the whole thing upside down. It is a good idea to ease the pudding from the sides of the basin with a knife first. Put on the table and serve immediately.

Apple Charlotte

This is a classic that never fails to impress. It has to be made with Bramley apples. If you don't want to use apples, try rhubarb or a mix of apples and rhubarb. You could make it in one large dish (when it would take 30-40 minutes to cook) or four small ones, as here. Chuck custard, double cream or ice-cream on it and dive in.

Serves 4

1 kg (2¼lb) Bramley apples
juice of 1 lemon
175g (6oz) unsalted butter
125g (4½oz) caster sugar
4 tbsp smooth apricot jam
10 thin slices white bread,
    crusts removed

1   Preheat the oven to 180°C/350°F/gas mark 4.

2   Peel, core and slice the apples, place them in a bowl and pour over the lemon juice.

3   In a large pan, melt 25g (1oz) of the butter, then add the sugar, apples and any lemon juice. Put the lid on and cook over a gentle heat for about 10 minutes, stirring occasionally.

4   Remove the lid and cook for a further 5-10 minutes, until you have a smooth purée. Add the apricot jam and allow to cool.

5   Meanwhile, melt the remaining butter. Cut the slices of bread in half, and then cut each half into 4 slices to get small fingers. Dip each piece of bread into the melted butter and use to line 4 small dariole moulds about 6cm (2½in) wide. Reserve some slices, dipped in butter, for lids.

6   Once the moulds are lined, spoon in the apple purée and top with the remaining bread slices. Bake for 15 minutes, or until golden on top.

7   Remove from the oven and allow to cool slightly. Carefully turn out and serve immediately.

Cheat's Raspberry and Cassis Ripple Ice-cream

When serving this, hide the ice-cream cartons to make it look like you did it all yourself. It's tastes fantastic!

Serves 8

2 litres (3½ pints) vanilla
   ice-cream, partly thawed in the
   fridge until just soft

CASSIS SAUCE
300g (10½oz) frozen raspberries
25g (1oz) caster sugar
juice and finely grated zest of
   ½ lemon
3 tbsp cassis

1   To make the sauce, blend the raspberries, sugar, lemon juice and zest and cassis. Pass it through a sieve to remove the raspberry seeds.

2   Drizzle the sauce over the ice-cream and quickly marble it through, using a folding motion with a spoon.

3   Place the ice-cream in a freezer-proof container and freeze it for 3-4 hours before serving.

Blood Orange Ice-cream

The custard base here could be used for other ice-creams: add a little vanilla extract for a vanilla ice or some other fruit flavourings. You could also add some brandy to this custard for a brandy sauce for Christmas pud.

Serves 6

500g (1lb 2oz) blood oranges,
   preferably unwaxed
350g (12oz) caster sugar
6 medium egg yolks
200ml (7fl oz) double cream
400ml (14fl oz) full-fat milk

1   Finely grate the orange zest into a bowl, then quarter the fruits. Put the quarters into the bowl as well, and pour over 250g (9oz) of the caster sugar. Refrigerate, covered, for a day or so.

2   Squeeze the juice from the mixture – start by using your hands, then press through a nylon sieve. Measure the juice and discard the pulp.

3   Make the custard for the ice-cream by whisking the egg yolks and remaining sugar together until thick and pale. This should take 10 minutes in a food mixer.

4   Bring the cream and milk to the boil in heavy-bottomed pan, then whisk this into the eggs. Return the pan to the heat and cook gently, stirring constantly, until the custard begins to thicken. Do not allow the mixture to boil or it will scramble. If you prefer, you can cook the custard in a bowl set over a pan of simmering water. Check whether it is thick enough by coating the back of a wooden spoon with it; if, when you slide your finger through it, it leaves a trail, it is ready. Remove from the heat and cool.

5   Whisk the juice with $1\frac{1}{2}$ times its volume of cooled custard, then churn in an ice-cream maker. Alternatively, pour the mixture into freezer-proof containers and half-freeze, then whisk again to remove the ice crystals. Return to the freezer.

TARTS

I've had some very happy times as a pastry chef – particularly inventing
(and tasting) new tarts! This chapter includes some of my favourites.
Believe me, home-made pastry is incredibly easy to make and tastes a
million times nicer than the shop-bought stuff. My recommendation is that
you make enough pastry for two flan rings, and then bung one in the
freezer – it freezes brilliantly.

Sweet Shortcrust Pastry

Making pastry may seem like hard work, but it's worth it. It's not just that the flavour and texture are better than that of the shop-bought stuff – it makes you feel good, too. It makes me think of my gran, who never overworked the dough or used too much flour (which can toughen it and make it shrink when cooking).

**Lines a 23cm (9in) diameter,
3cm (1½in) deep flan ring**

115g (4oz) cold unsalted butter, cubed
225g (8oz) plain white flour
a pinch of salt
2 tbsp caster sugar
2 tbsp ground almonds
1 egg, lightly beaten, plus extra to glaze

Note: It's a good idea to double the quantity to line two flan rings, so you can use one and put the other in the freezer.

1 Place the butter, flour, salt, sugar and almonds in a food processor. Blitz until you have a fine breadcrumb texture, but do not overwork. Add the egg and ½ an egg-shell full of cold water and mix well, using the pulse button until the pastry balls; again, do not overwork.

2 Turn the pastry out of the processor and knead very gently, just to bring it together. If you have doubled the mixture, divide the pastry in two. Flatten each piece of dough slightly (this makes it easier to roll when chilled) and wrap in cling-film, then chill in the fridge for at least 20 minutes – an hour or two would be better.

3 Grease your tart tin. Lightly flour the work surface. Roll the pastry out so you end up with a circle about 4cm (1½in) larger in diameter than the flan ring. Carefully roll the pastry on to the rolling pin and then unroll it over the flan ring, taking care not stretch the pastry too much.

4 Immediately ease the pastry into the ring and use your thumb to gently push it into the bottom and corners of the ring; do not leave any creases in the outside or air between the pastry and the ring. Leave about 1cm (½in) overhanging the top edge of the ring. Then trim off with a sharp knife or roll a rolling pin over the top to remove the excess. Use your thumb to squeeze up the top edge again (the pastry will shrink back a little during cooking), and pinch with your thumb and forefinger to make the edge more decorative. Using a piece of well-floured leftover pastry, push the bottom of the flan into the corners so it's nice and flush. Chill for 30 minutes. Preheat the oven to 200°C/400°F/gas mark 6.

5 Cut out a round piece of greaseproof paper 4cm (1½in) larger than the flan and place it inside the pastry-lined flan tin. Fill with baking beans and blind bake for 15 minutes, or until the top edge is slightly brown. Remove the paper and beans, turn the oven down to 160°C/325°F/gas mark 3, and cook for a further 10 minutes, until the pastry is set but has taken no colour. Remove from the oven, brush with beaten egg (to stop the pastry getting soggy when you add the filling), and then put it back in the oven for 2 minutes to seal. Cool for a little while before adding the filling.

When you first turn the pastry out of the processor, gently knead it.

Flatten the pastry slightly, wrap it, then chill it for at least 20 minutes.

Roll out the pastry on a lightly floured work surface.

You need a circle 4cm (1½in) bigger than your tart ring.

Push the pastry into the bottom and corners of the ring.

Line the pastry case with greaseproof and pour in baking beans.

Bitter Chocolate Tart

You need the best chocolate for pastries, but don't listen to chefs who tell you to use over 70 per cent cocoa solids. The max you need is 70 per cent, otherwise you can't eat the stuff. Serve this tart warm and never refrigerate it once cooked. To make it even more special, make a chocolate pastry case: substitute 35g (1¼oz) of the flour with cocoa powder.

Serves 6-8

200g (7oz) bitter chocolate, 70% cocoa solids (no more)
100g (3½oz) milk chocolate
2 large eggs, plus 2 large egg yolks, at room temperature
60g (2¼oz) caster sugar
150g (5½oz) unsalted butter, melted
1 x 23cm (9in) plain or chocolate sweet shortcrust pastry case, baked blind (see page 76)
icing sugar

COFFEE BEAN SYRUP
2 tbsp liquid glucose
10 fresh coffee beans, crushed
200g (7oz) caster sugar
juice of ½ lemon

1   Preheat the oven to 220°C/425°F/gas mark 7.

2   Break the 2 chocolates into pieces, and melt together in a heatproof bowl over a pan of gently simmering water.

3   Place the eggs, egg yolks and sugar in the bowl of a food mixer and whisk at high speed until very thick. Remove the bowl from the machine and carefully stir in the melted chocolate, taking care not to knock too much air out of the eggs. Fold in the melted butter, again very carefully.

4   Place the blind-baked flan case on a baking sheet, pour the chocolate mixture into the pastry shell, and bake for 7-8 minutes, or until just set – do not let the edges soufflé up. Remove from the oven and leave to cool on a wire rack.

5   Meanwhile, make the coffee bean syrup. Place 225ml (8fl oz) cold water, the glucose, coffee beans and sugar in a pan and bring to the boil. Remove from the heat, cover and allow to cool. Finally, add lemon juice to taste to the cooled syrup, then strain to remove the coffee beans.

6   Eat the tart at room temperature, cut into wedges, dusted heavily with icing sugar, accompanied by the coffee syrup.

Quick Chocolate Tart

As you can see by the number of chocolate tarts I've included in this book, it's one of my favourite things to eat! This one is quite quick to prepare, but looks and tastes no less special because of that.

Serves 12

PASTRY

255g (9oz) unsalted butter, softened
40g (1½oz) icing sugar
1 medium egg
500g (1lb 2oz) plain flour, sifted

CHOCOLATE FILLING

350ml (12fl oz) double cream
140ml (¼ pint) full fat milk
400g (14oz) dark chocolate (at least 70% cocoa solids), broken into pieces
3 medium eggs, beaten

1 Preheat the oven to 180°C/350°F/gas mark 4. Place a baking sheet on the middle shelf in the oven.

2 Cream the butter and sugar in a food mixer, or in a bowl with a wooden spoon, until pale and fluffy, then add the egg.

3 Turn the food mixer to its lowest setting and add the plain flour. Mix until the pastry comes together. Wrap in cling-film and chill for at least 30 minutes.

4 Butter a 20cm (8in) tart ring or loose-bottomed tart tin. Roll out the pastry into a circle 3mm (⅛in) thick and about 5cm (2in) bigger than the tart ring. Line the tart ring with the pastry, pressing it down gently and leaving a 2.5cm (1in) overhang.

5 Prick the base with a fork and blind bake for 20 minutes, or until starting to brown. Remove and trim the overhanging pastry level with the top of the ring, using a sharp, heavy knife.

6 Turn the oven down to 130°C/250°F/gas mark ½. To make the filling, in a saucepan heat the cream and milk until trembling, just under boiling point. Take off the heat. Add the chocolate to the cream and milk and stir until fully blended, then add the beaten eggs and mix again.

7 Pour the chocolate mixture into the tart case and bake for about 1 hour. The tart is done when it is still a bit wobbly in the middle. Leave to set for at least 45 minutes before serving. Serve with the orange ice-cream on page 73.

Pecan Pie

I find this quite hard to cook, as it appears to be cooked long before it is. If you're unsure, turn the oven a bit lower and cook for a while longer or else the nuts will burn.

Serves 8

350g (12oz) pecans (or walnuts)
55g (2oz) bitter chocolate, grated
1 tsp vanilla extract
2 pinches salt
350ml (12fl oz) good maple syrup
4 large eggs
300g (10½oz) granulated sugar
115g (4oz) unsalted butter, melted
1 x 23cm (9in) sweet shortcrust
   pastry case, baked blind (*see* page 76)

1 Preheat the oven to 170°C/325°F/gas mark 3.

2 Place the nuts, grated chocolate, vanilla extract, salt and maple syrup in a bowl. Beat the eggs in a separate bowl, then stir into the nut mixture together with the sugar. Finally add the melted butter and stir well.

3 Pour into the prepared pastry case and bake for 55-60 minutes, or until set in the middle. Allow to cool completely before cutting.

HALLOWE'EN AND BONFIRE NIGHT

I have so many brilliant memories of Hallowe'en and Bonfire Night when I was a kid – running down the hill to see the fireworks and get one of granny's baked potatoes, scoffing my auntie's toffee from a waxed bag, and cooking marshmallows on the bonfire. Nothing could beat it!

Spicy Bean Stew with Sausages

Most adults and kids love this because it's so simple to make. Onions and garlic are used as a base, and good-quality sausages are the key. Cut them up into pieces, fry them all, add some canned beans and tomatoes, and stew down for about 15 minutes. Beautiful! I served this at a truckers' café once, but for breakfast, and 150 of them woofed it down!

Serves 4

5 tbsp olive or vegetable oil
8 good free-range pork sausages
4 streaky bacon rashers, chopped
1 medium onion, peeled and
   chopped
2 garlic cloves, peeled and
   chopped
1 red chilli, chopped (or more if it
   is really cold!)
1 tbsp soft brown sugar
2 x 400g cans plum or chopped
   tomatoes
a dash of red/white wine
   (whatever is open)
2 x 300g cans cannellini beans,
   drained and rinsed
1 x 300g can kidney beans,
   drained and rinsed
leaves from small bunch of fresh
   parsley, chopped
salt and freshly ground black
   pepper

1   Place a large heavy-based saucepan on the hob and heat 3 tbsp of the oil. Add the sausages and fry over a medium heat, turning them over until they are browned on the outside. Take them out of the pan and chop them into 4cm (1½in) pieces. Set them aside on a plate.

2   Add the remaining oil to the pan, turn the heat down to low, add the bacon and onion, and fry gently for around 10 minutes, stirring from time to time so that they don't catch on the bottom. They will pick up all the lovely sausagey goo in the bottom of the pan.

3   Add the garlic and chilli and fry for another couple of minutes, then add the brown sugar. Pour in the tomatoes, wine and 300ml (10fl oz) water, then stir in the sausage pieces along with the beans, and cook for 15-20 minutes over a low-medium heat.

4   Stir in the chopped parsley, salt and lots of black pepper, and serve with some nice fresh crusty bread or mashed potato.

Roast Squash, Lemon and Mustard Purée

This is a good dish to serve with roast meat, poultry or game, and makes a nice change from mashed spuds every time.

Serves 6-8

2 butternut squashes, about 650g (1lb 7oz) each

2 garlic cloves, peeled and crushed

2 lemons, each cut into 4 slices

1 tbsp olive oil

1 sprig fresh thyme, leaves picked off

90g (3¼oz) unsalted butter

3 tbsp coarse-grain mustard

5 tbsp double cream

salt and freshly ground black pepper

1 Preheat the oven to 190°C/375°F/gas mark 5.

2 Cut the squashes in half, scoop out the seeds, then peel and chop the flesh into even-sized chunks. Place the squash in a bowl with the garlic, lemons, oil and thyme.

3 Melt 55g (2oz) of the butter and add half of this to the bowl. Toss together, then spread out in a roasting tin and roast for about 20 minutes, until the squash feels tender when pierced with a knife.

4 Scoop the squash into a food processor with the remaining melted butter, the mustard, cream and seasoning. Whiz to a smooth purée. Alternatively, mash the squash and stir in the other ingredients.

5 Reheat and dot with the remaining butter when ready to serve.

Treacle Toffee

My auntie used to make toffee, which she served in a waxed bag, for Bonfire Night. This was really popular with all the kids! I think she learnt the recipe from my great-great-grandmother, who had a corner shop selling toffee and fudge. My auntie would make a variety of toffees – some with raisins or sultanas, some plain, some with syrup and some, of course, with black treacle. To break it up, she used an old toffee hammer that she got from Terry's Chocolates, when my father was manager of their restaurant in York (now sadly shut down). She always made it nice and soft, probably because she never fridged it. The toffee was kept in the biscuit tin with the commemorative plaque of Queen Elizabeth from when she got married, a tin which I treasure to this day. My auntie sadly passed away about 15 years ago, but the legacy of her toffee remains.

Makes about 800g (1³⁄₄lb)

450g (1lb) demerara sugar
85g (3oz) unsalted butter, softened
¹⁄₂ tsp cream of tartar
100g (3¹⁄₂oz) black treacle
100g (3¹⁄₂oz) golden syrup
a handful of sultanas

1   Place the sugar in a heavy-bottomed saucepan with 150ml (5fl oz) water and heat until all the sugar has dissolved. Add the rest of the ingredients, apart from the sultanas, and put in a sugar thermometer.

2   Bring to the boil, brushing the sides of the pan down with a pastry brush dipped in water to stop crystals forming. Do not stir. When the sugar reaches 132°C/270°F, quickly and carefully fold in the sultanas. Pour the mixture into a greaseproof-paper-lined 18cm (7in) tin and allow to cool. When set, break into pieces and store in a jar.

Toffee Apples

The first secret of good toffee apples is to get a nice apple. Make sure the apples are dry, or else the caramel won't stick. It's also important to add enough butter to your caramel.

Makes 4

8 small, dry eating apples
toffee (as above, but replacing the treacle with another 100g/3¹⁄₂oz golden syrup, increasing the butter to 115g/4oz and omitting the sultanas)

1   Make the toffee as above. When you reach the sultana stage (omitting the sultanas), stick a fork in each apple (forks are much better than sticks) and dip it into the caramel.

2   Immediately put the apple on a lightly oiled work surface or non-stick tray. Repeat with all the apples. Leave until cool and the toffee has set.

CHRISTMAS BAKING

Don't you just love Christmas baking? All those fantastic smells of dried fruit and booze – and a really good excuse to have a sneaky drink while you work! I recommend making everything yourself, including the marzipan for your Christmas cake. Go on, you'll be glad you tried it!

Marzipan (Almond Paste)

For some reason people still buy ready-made marzipan, particularly the fluorescent yellow stuff, which they then put on the Christmas cake they've spent ages making. Why, when marzipan can so easily be made at home?

Covers a 20cm (8in) cake

225g (8oz) icing sugar, plus extra
   for dusting
500g (1lb 2oz) ground almonds
1 large egg (weighing about
   75g/2³/₄oz)
3-4 tsp lemon juice

GLAZE
1 tbsp apricot jam

1   Sift the sugar into a bowl and mix in the almonds. Beat the egg well, then add it and the lemon juice to the dry ingredients. Using a wooden spoon, beat to a firm paste, then knead on a work surface that has been sprinkled with icing sugar. (If you don't find most marzipan too sweet, add another 225g/8oz sugar and use 2 medium eggs instead of 1 large.)

2   Slice the top from the cake to make it even, then turn it upside down and put it on a wire rack. Boil the jam and 1 tbsp water in a small pan, sieve it into a bowl and, while it is hot, brush some over the top (what was the bottom) of the cake.

3   Set aside a third of the marzipan and roll out the rest to a circle a little larger than the cake – do this on a sheet of clean greaseproof and use the cake tin as a guide. Press the glazed side of the cake down on to the marzipan. Remove the paper and smooth the marzipan over the sides.

4   Measure the depth of the cake and its circumference. Roll out the remaining marzipan to these measurements, again on a sheet of greaseproof. Brush the cake sides with the remaining hot apricot glaze and roll it slowly along the strip of marzipan. Pat everything into place, closing the cracks, and put the cake back on its rack.

Royal Icing

Covers a 20cm (8in) cake

4 small egg whites
4 tsp lemon juice
1kg (2 ¹/₄ lb) icing sugar, sifted

1   Whisk the egg whites until they are white and foamy but not stiff. Stir in the lemon juice, then the sugar, bit by bit, using a wooden spoon. When everything is combined, continue to beat the mixture until it is a dazzling white. Cover the basin and leave for an hour before using.

2   To ice the cake, have a bowl of hot water handy. Put half the icing on the cake, dip the palette knife into the hot water (it shouldn't be too wet), then use it to spread the icing. Cover the cake, then put on the remaining icing, either roughly to make a snowy effect or with the aid of a forcing bag and nozzles. Leave for at least 2 days to set before eating.

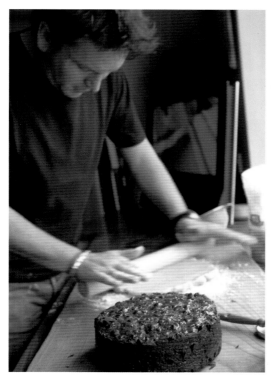

Roll out the marzipan – it is easier to do this on greaseproof paper.

Brush the cake with glaze, then place the marzipan on top.

Either pat the sides down or roll a separate piece for the sides.

Use a palette knife to get a rough, snowy effect with the icing.

Real Christmas Bread

There are many variations of Christmas breads, from country to country. This is my version, and it was invented purely because so often at Christmas we find we've quite a lot of mincemeat left over. It's very simple to make and uses few ingredients. I use fresh yeast, but if you can't find it, use dried (read the instructions on the packet).

Makes 1 loaf

500g (1lb 2oz) strong white flour, plus extra for dusting
100g (3½oz) mincemeat (bought or home-made, *see* page 116)
finely grated zest and juice of 2 oranges
finely grated zest and juice of 2 lemons
55g (2oz) unsalted butter
10g (¼oz) salt
25g (1oz) fresh yeast
280ml (9½fl oz) warm water

1   Place the flour, mincemeat, citrus zest and juice, butter, salt and yeast in a large bowl and mix together. Gradually mix in the warm water to form a dough.

2   Place the dough on a lightly floured surface and knead for 4 minutes. Shape into a rough sausage shape, around 15cm (6in) across. Place on a baking sheet lined with baking parchment and leave aside to rise for 1 hour, covered with a tea-towel.

3   Preheat the oven to 220°C/425°F/gas mark 7.

4   Slash the top of the loaf with a knife and dust with flour. Bake for 25 minutes, until golden brown and hollow when tapped. Cool on a wire rack.

Gran's Madeira Cake

My auntie used to make this simple and classic cake at least three times a week. Not only was it my grandad's favourite cake (the recipe came from my gran) but my uncles and I would dive into the tin at least once a day. There was never much left for my sister, only the crumbs at the bottom!

Makes 1 x 20cm (8in) cake

175g (6oz) unsalted butter, diced, plus extra for greasing
225g (8oz) self-raising flour, plus extra for dusting
175g (6oz) caster sugar
3 large eggs
30g (1¼oz) ground almonds
juice and finely grated zest of 1 lemon
2 tbsp milk

1 Preheat the oven to 180°C/350°F/gas mark 4. Use some extra butter and flour to grease and dust a 20cm (8in) square tin (or line with greaseproof). You could also use 2 x 450g (1lb) loaf tins.

2 Place the butter in the bowl of a food processor with the sugar, and blend to a light-coloured cream, scraping down the sides when needed. While the machine is running, add the eggs one by one, being careful not to split the mixture. If this happens, add a little of the flour to bring it together, but try not to get it to that stage as this will tighten up the mixture and make your cake less light and airy.

3 Add the almonds, flour, lemon juice and zest, and milk and blend quickly for 10 seconds on maximum to a smooth batter.

4 Pour the mixture into the prepared tin and bake in the bottom of the oven for 60-70 minutes (the smaller cakes for 40-45 minutes).

5 Leave to cool before storing in an airtight tin. However, if it comes out like my auntie's cakes used to, it won't be in there for long.

Traditional Mincemeat

I know you're going to look at this recipe with horror because of the raw mince I've used in it. But this is the traditional way of making mincemeat. Most bought mincemeat doesn't have meat in it, of course, but I thought it would be interesting to explore. You can easily omit the steak if you want to.

Makes loads

225g (8oz) seedless raisins
350g (12oz) currants
175g (6oz) good lean rump steak, minced
350g (12oz) beef suet, chopped
225g (8oz) dark brown sugar
15g (½oz) candied citron peel, chopped
15g (½oz) candied lemon peel, chopped
15g (½oz) candied orange peel, chopped
¼ small nutmeg, grated
finely grated zest and juice of ½ lemon
350g (12oz) apples, weighed after peeling and coring, finely chopped
75ml (2½fl oz) brandy

1   Mix all the ingredients together in the order given, pouring in the brandy when everything else is well mixed together.

2   Press closely into sterilized jars to exclude the air. Cover and leave for at least a fortnight.

CHRISTMAS DAY

Christmas Day was magical when we were kids, wasn't it? The smell of spices and of the bird cooking, the twinkling lights, the presents hidden all over the house. Now I'm grown up, the excitement of Christmas is in recreating that magic for friends and their kids – in particular by cooking some delicious classic Christmas food!

Countdown to Christmas

Christmas is one of my favourite times of the year. I remember getting so excited when I was a young lad: the house was full of spicy smells; a fragrant tree hung with apples; Christmas lights and home-made biscuits dominated the sitting room; mysterious, brightly coloured parcels appeared in every corner; and then there was the ritual of hanging my stocking on the fireplace and leaving a mince pie and glass of brandy for Santa Claus.

Nowadays, the excitement is still there, but it has changed direction a little. Now I look forward to cooking up a storm, to being surrounded by family and friends, and to eating and drinking – both of which I probably do far too much!

However much we look forward to the festive season, quite a few of us combine the excitement with a sense of dread, because it always seems to involve so much buying, cooking and preparation. It's become almost like cooking for a siege. Your Christmas holiday may last only three or so days, or it may stretch to over a week. Either way, it can be a little difficult, particularly if you have a lot of people to cater for. It all comes down to good planning. The first thing to do is make a list, and you should do this some months in advance if you feel like it, because there are several elements of the traditional Christmas that can be planned and made well ahead.

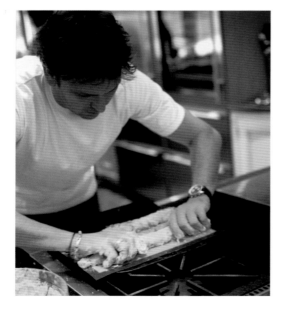

Two months in advance

The sweet centrepieces of Christmas eating are the Christmas pudding, the cake and mincemeat, and all of these can be prepared well in advance of the big day.

The traditional time for making the pudding is Stir-up Sunday, around the 30 November, although I have made some as early as August. The cake can be made six weeks or so in advance, but remember to moisten it at some point with more alcohol. Both will survive well so long as they are well wrapped and kept in a cool place.

The mincemeat can be made up to two months in advance. Any other preserves will taste even better if made early and allowed a good time to mature: you will need the savoury ones for accompanying the inevitable leftover cold meats, the sweet ones for Christmas breakfasts and teas.

Think, too, about less obvious things that could be frozen for use at Christmas: stocks (good for soups, gravies and sauces), soups (always handy for a lunch or late-night snack) and ice-creams. You can freeze home-made or bought pastry for the mince pies and any canapés you might want. Basics such as butter, milk (in plastic bottles), sausage-meat and sausages can also be bought and frozen.

One month in advance

This is when you have to work your hardest. Now is the time to check your basic supplies. Have you enough flour and sugar? Is the flour past its sell-by date? How long have your powdered spices been sitting there? Buy new if necessary, for spices and flour can deteriorate over time. Have you got enough risotto rice (for a lunchtime risotto, one of the handiest recipes for times like this), basmati or other rice to go with the turkey curry? You will have plenty of leftovers, so you need basics to use with them. If you have particular baking in mind, buy foods like pistachios, dried apricots, prunes and pine nuts.

Ordering is the order of the day

Make your list for your butcher – turkey or goose, ham, sausages, bacon, eggs, sausage-meat, etc. You can collect these a day or two before Christmas, and ordering well in advance gives him plenty of time to organize himself. I would always go for a free-range turkey.

Give a list of your needs to the fishmonger as well. And if you have a good deli nearby, order any preserved meats you want, such as sliced Parma ham, well in advance (they can slice just before you come in, and you won't have to wait when you collect them).

You'll need to contact your alcohol supplier, too, for wines of both colours, Champagne or a sparkling wine (good for buck's fizz on the big morning), brandy or rum (for the Christmas pudding butter or sauce), other spirits of choice, mixers, beers, soft drinks and waters. Choose a supplier that will deliver.

Your greengrocer will appreciate a list of what you need, and he can make up a box for you to collect at the last minute: potatoes, onions, green vegetables, etc. Try to choose seasonally, and I would always go for the organic stuff. Brussels are traditional, but don't forget about red cabbage, leeks, parsnips, fennel, sweet potatoes and Jerusalem artichokes, and all the salad leaves you will need to go with the cold meats.

Fruit and nuts should be seasonal as well: oranges and tangerines (the former for juicing and the latter for the tip of the Christmas stocking!), Cox's apples, dried figs, nuts, chestnuts and dates. Christmas is also a good time to have a little exotic fruit around too, pineapple, mango or pawpaw, for instance (these are great for breakfast).

If you have a good local baker, it might be a good idea to order some bread from him: many's the time I've gone in at the last minute and his shelves were bare!

There's quite a lot of cooking that can be done in the last couple of weeks before the holiday. You could make a Stollen (*see* page 110, wrap it well) or the marzipan for the more traditional Christmas cake (keep wrapped in the fridge). You could make up some uncooked pastry canapés, and open-freeze them: they can just be popped in the oven when you need them. And you could make and freeze a fresh cranberry sauce.

One week in advance

Check, check and double-check that everything has been organized.

This is when you could be buying everyday things that are not covered in other areas – crisps, last-minute presents, candles, crackers, Christmas paper napkins, more wrapping paper (I never buy enough).

You could make a pâté or terrine a few days before. It will last well if it is wrapped up and kept in the fridge.

You could make a royal icing for your cake a couple of days before using it, but allow two to three days after icing for it to set.

Christmas Eve

You don't want to be doing too much on Christmas Eve! This is the day for collection and delivery, from the butcher, the baker, the fishmonger, the vintner, the candlestickmaker…. So you have to make sure you or someone else is around.

If you do have to wait in for something, and you can't settle to a movie or a good book, you can still keep yourself busy. Make some mince pies or tarts or brandy snaps (they'll keep well in an airtight tin until you want to stuff them with cream); make the brandy butter or sauce, and prepare the stuffing and the giblet stock.

You could even prepare the vegetables the evening before. I know it's not ideal, but it will save you time on the day. Keep peeled potatoes and parsnips in water.

Turkey with Orange, Rosemary and Gravy

The most common mistake people make when they roast turkey is the timing, especially at Christmas. With the kids running around and the gravy boiling over, you tend to forget about it! Calculate 18 minutes per 450g (1lb). Leave the turkey to rest well before you carve it, and never use an electric carving knife, as this will rip the meat and make it tough.

Serves 10-12

1 x 4.5-5.4kg (10-12lb) turkey,
　giblets removed
2 oranges
24 large rosemary sprigs
55g (2oz) unsalted butter, at room
　temperature
coarse sea salt and freshly ground
　black pepper
22 streaky bacon rashers

GRAVY
600ml (1 pint) chicken stock or
　water
300ml (10fl oz) white wine or
　water
3 tbsp plain flour
2 tsp Dijon mustard

1   Preheat the oven to 190°C/375°F/gas mark 5. Wash the turkey inside and out and dry well with kitchen paper. Quarter 1 orange and put the quarters in the cavity with 2 rosemary sprigs. If you are stuffing the turkey, put the stuffing in the neck-end only, pushing it up towards the breast (don't pull the neck skin too tightly, as the stuffing expands during cooking). Secure the neck-end with skewers crossways, then tie the turkey legs together at the top of the drumsticks for a good shape.

2   Weigh the turkey and calculate the cooking time at 18 minutes per 450g (1lb). Grease a large roasting tin with a little butter. Put the turkey in the tin. Melt the remaining butter. Halve the remaining orange and squeeze one-half over the turkey, then mix the remaining juice with the melted butter. Brush some of this butter over the turkey skin and season (keep the rest for basting later). Cover the turkey with foil and roast for the calculated time. Brush it every hour with the orange-butter mixture. An hour before the end of the cooking time, remove the foil. If you want, you can bung the oven up a bit higher. The turkey is ready if the juices run clear when the thickest part of the leg is pierced with a knife

3   For each rosemary and bacon spikes, lay a bacon rasher on the work surface with a rosemary sprig on top. Wrap the bacon around the sprig and lay it on a baking sheet with the join underneath.

4   Remove the turkey from the oven and transfer it to a platter, tightly cover with foil, and allow to rest for up to 30 minutes before carving, leaving the oven on. Put the bacon and rosemary spikes in the oven 20 minutes before you are ready to serve, and cook until the bacon is crisp.

5   While the turkey is resting, pour off all but 6 tbsp of the juices from the roasting tin into a large jug and leave them to settle. When the fat has risen to the surface, spoon it off and make the darker juices underneath up to 600ml (1 pint) with water or stock, then add the wine. Heat the juices in the roasting tin on the hob. Stir in the flour, scraping up the bits from the bottom of the tin, and cook, stirring, to a nutty brown. Slowly pour in the liquid, then bring to the boil and keep stirring until thickened. Season with the mustard and salt and pepper.

6   Serve the bird with the spikes, roasties, and whatever else you want.

Brussels Sprouts with Chestnuts and Bacon

A simple way to make Brussels taste more interesting – although if you use Brussels still on the vine (much more readily available now), the sprouts don't dry out so much and are fresher in flavour. Chestnuts are readily available in cans or vacuumm-packed from delis and supermarkets. If buying a can, look carefully to make sure it is a savoury version.

Serves 10-12

1.3kg (3lb) Brussels sprouts, or 2 stems Brussels sprouts, trimmed
salt and freshly ground black pepper
a large knob of unsalted butter
12 smoked streaky bacon rashers or dry-cured ham, cut in thin matchsticks
1 x 200g pack cooked, peeled whole chestnuts (vacuum-packed)

1 Bring a large pan of salted water to the boil, add the sprouts and cook until just tender, 8-12 minutes, depending on their size. Drain well.

2 Meanwhile, melt the butter in a large frying pan or wok and fry the bacon until crisp. Add the chestnuts and cook for about a minute, to heat through.

3 When warm, tip in the drained Brussels. Mix well and season with salt and pepper.

Roast Potatoes

Everyone has a different recipe for roast potatoes, but this is mine. It was my gran's first, then my mother's, and it's still the best. Use lard or dripping for the cooking fat (or vegetable oil if you don't have either), but best of all use some goose fat.

Serves 6

10 medium King Edward, Maris
   Piper or Desirée potatoes
a good pinch of salt
50g (1¾oz) fat (*see* above)

1 Preheat the oven to 200°C/400°F/gas mark 6. Peel the potatoes and cut each one in half (into 3 if large). Place in a saucepan, cover with cold water and add the salt. Bring to the boil and simmer for a maximum of 3-4 minutes. Put into a colander and allow to drain well.

2 Heat the lard or dripping in a roasting tray on the stove, and fry the potatoes until they start to brown. Turn them occasionally. Sprinkle generously with salt, then roast for about 30 minutes.

3 Remove from the oven and turn the potatoes in the tray in order to prevent them from sticking. Roast for another 30 minutes and remove. Serve immediately. (I also love roast potatoes cold – which is why I always make bucketloads of them! I eat them with cold meat and a good wodge of butter.)

Roast Parsnips

I love these, at Christmas or any other time of the year.

Serves 6

900g (2lb) parsnips, peeled and
   quartered
2 tbsp olive oil
2 fresh thyme sprigs, leaves
   picked off
salt and freshly ground black
   pepper
40g (1½oz) unsalted butter
4-6 tbsp runny honey

1 Preheat the oven to 200°C/400°F/gas mark 6. If the parsnips are large and have woody centres, cut these out before cooking. The parsnips can be boiled in salted water for 2 minutes before roasting.

2 Preheat a roasting tray on the stove and add the oil. Fry the parsnips until golden on all sides, allowing burnt tinges on the edges. Add the thyme and roast, turning every 10 minutes, for 20-30 minutes.

3 Remove from the oven and season. Add the butter and honey. Return to the oven for 5-10 minutes. Place in a serving dish and spoon over juices.

Sausage and Bacon Wraps with Sage and Honey

Just look at them bubbling away in the pan: a lovely mixture of sausage and bacon. Buy dry-cured bacon so that when you fry it you don't get that weeping white liquid coming out the bacon (from the water injected into so much bacon these days). Both sausage and bacon will end up being nice and crisp and brown.

Serves 4

8 streaky bacon rashers
16 cocktail sausages
16 small fresh sage leaves
2 tbsp runny honey

1   Preheat the oven to 180°C/350°F/gas mark 4. Cut each of the bacon rashers in half.

2   Roll up the sausages in the bacon with a small sage leaf. Secure with a wooden cocktail stick if you like (it's not entirely necessary), and arrange in a shallow tin. Drizzle with the runny honey.

3   Place in the oven while the turkey or goose is resting, and cook at 180°C/350°F/gas mark 4 for 25-30 minutes. Turn over once or twice to brown evenly all over. Remove the cocktail sticks before serving, if necessary.

Quick Christmas Pudding with Baked Ice-cream

This is a great way of saving time on Christmas Day. The ice-cream parcels are better made in advance (at least the day before) and placed in the freezer. The icing sugar on the top caramelizes to create a lovely crunchy garnish for the hot Christmas pudding.

Serves 4

8 filo pastry sheets
1 medium egg, beaten
4 scoops bought or home-made
    vanilla ice-cream
icing sugar
4 x 115g small Christmas puddings
200ml (7fl oz) brandy sauce (see
    opposite)
4 fresh mint sprigs

1 Preheat the oven to 220°C/425°F/gas mark 7.

2 Unroll the filo and cut into 12 x 10cm (4in) squares. Layer 3 of the squares at slight alternate angles and brush with some beaten egg.

3 Place a scoop of the ice-cream in the centre of each filo square, and bring up the sides of the pastry to stick together. Brush with beaten egg.

4 If cooking straight away, dust with icing sugar, place on an oven tray and bake for about 3-4 minutes. Alternatively, place in the freezer until ready to use (much better).

5 Meanwhile, place the puddings in the microwave to cook (follow packet instructions) and warm the brandy sauce through on the stove.

6 Spoon the warm sauce into the centre of the plates, and place a Christmas pudding in the middle. Remove the ice-cream parcel from the oven and place on top of the pudding.

7 To finish, simply dust the top with icing sugar and garnish with a sprig of mint. Serve immediately.

Brandy Sauce

This is one of the few recipes I use granulated sugar in. As you can probably imagine, it was used in my grandmother's recipe (although she had to grate sugar from the large lump or chop sugar cubes). I remember her bringing this sauce back home to the farmhouse, and fighting with my sister to remove the greaseproof paper from the top.

Serves 4-6

200ml (7fl oz) double cream
600ml (1 pint) full-fat milk
25g (1oz) cornflour, slaked with
    4 tbsp cold water
55g (2oz) unrefined granulated
    sugar
55g (2oz) unsalted butter, cubed
brandy, to taste

1 Bring the cream and milk to the boil together, and then stir in the slaked cornflour. Bring back to the boil, stirring, to thicken.

2 Remove from the heat and stir in the sugar and butter, until dissolved. Finally, stir in brandy to taste.

3 Cover to stop a skin forming, and keep warm.

Christmas Pudding Ice-cream

This is a simple way of using leftover Christmas pudding. Please invest in a decent ice-cream maker, which blends while it is freezing. Make sure Father Christmas comes down the chimney with one! Serve the ice-cream with a large glass of brandy and brandy snaps.

Serves 4-6

85g (3oz) leftover Christmas
    pudding, chopped into small
    pieces
2 tbsp brandy
140g (5oz) caster sugar
1 cinnamon stick
$\frac{1}{2}$ tsp ground mixed spice
225ml (8fl oz) custard base for
    ice-cream (*see* page 151)
150ml (5fl oz) double cream

1 Soak the Christmas pudding in the brandy.

2 To make the stock syrup, heat 150ml (5fl oz) water and the sugar together in a heavy-based pan until the sugar has melted, then simmer to reduce to 185ml ($6\frac{1}{2}$fl oz). Transfer to a small pan and add the cinnamon stick and mixed spice. Remove from the heat and leave to cool and infuse for 15 minutes.

3 Mix the custard with the cream. Strain the stock syrup to remove the cinnamon and add to the cream mixture. Mix in the Christmas pudding and brandy.

4 Churn in an ice-cream maker until thick and frozen, then transfer to a freezerproof container. Store in the freezer for up to a couple of weeks.

NEW YEAR'S DAY

No-one wants to be slaving away in the kitchen with a hang-over on New Year's Day, so you have two choices: make it easy or make sure you can prepare most of it in advance. Oh yes, and of course the food must feel special. Everything in this chapter fits that criteria!

Bloody Mary

The ultimate hangover cure! Make your own tomato juice or use tomato passata. The only other things you need are plenty of Tabasco, a good wedge of lemon and, most importantly, loads of ice cubes. That way you get the Bloody Mary chilled right down, which is perfect for those mornings after the night before.

Serves 1 (I like it strong!)

50ml (2fl oz) vodka
90ml (3fl oz) tomato juice (*see above*)
juice of ½ lemon
2-4 dashes Tabasco sauce
3 dashes Worcestershire sauce
freshly ground black pepper
ice cubes
1 lemon wedge

1 Place the vodka, tomato and lemon juices, Tabasco and Worcestershire sauces in a blender or a cocktail shaker and mix. Taste and season with black pepper and/or more of either sauce if needed.

2 Pour into a tall glass full of ice, and serve with the wedge of lemon on top of the glass.

Scrambled Eggs with Chilli and Crisp Streaky Bacon on Toast

Scrambled egg is so simple to make, but still people overcook it and end up with rubbery, gelatinized stuff on toast. To prevent this, add double cream halfway through the cooking while you whisk everything together in the pan. Be sure to use dry-cured bacon.

Serves 4

12 streaky bacon rashers
55g (2oz) unsalted butter
6 medium eggs, beaten
salt and ground black pepper
100ml (3½fl oz) double cream

TO SERVE

4 pieces sliced bread, toasted and buttered
1 green chilli, seeded and finely diced

1 Heat a sauté pan on a medium heat. Add the bacon with half the butter, and cook until crisp and golden brown, a few minutes only. Remove from the pan and keep warm.

2 Wipe the pan and return to the heat with the remaining butter. Season the eggs well with salt and pepper, then pour into the pan. Quickly mix the eggs with a whisk and, when half-cooked, add the cream, whisking all the time.

3 Just as the eggs are beginning to set, remove from the heat, and season again. Spoon on to the toast, with a scattering of chopped chilli on top and bacon on the side. Serve immediately.

Smoked Haddock with Poached Egg and Horseradish Mash

Most people don't think poached eggs can be prepared in advance, but they can: simply poach the egg, then place it into ice-cold water to cool down. When cold, pop it in the fridge. When you want the eggs, blanch them in boiling water for 30 seconds and place them on your haddock. This is particularly useful when serving breakfast for lots of people.

Serves 4

4 x 200g (7oz) pieces natural
  smoked haddock
850ml (1½ pints) full-fat milk
juice of 1 lemon
6 black peppercorns
a few fresh parsley stalks
salt and freshly ground black
  pepper
4 large eggs
150g (5½oz) fresh young spinach
  leaves, washed

HORSERADISH MASH
900g (2lb) King Edward or Maris
  Piper potatoes, peeled and
  chopped
100g (3½oz) unsalted butter
approx 200ml (7fl oz) full-fat
  milk, warmed
2 tbsp creamed horseradish

1   For the mash, cook the potatoes in boiling salted water until tender, about 15 minutes. Once cooked, drain well and, while hot but not wet, place back in the pan and return to the heat. Mash with the butter and the warm milk. Once you get the texture you want, beat in the horseradish and some salt and pepper to taste and keep warm.

2   For the haddock, put the milk, lemon juice, peppercorns, parsley stalks and a little salt into a medium-sized flat pan, and bring to a simmer. At the same time, place a pan of salted water on to boil for the eggs.

3   Add the haddock pieces to the simmering milk, and cook gently for about 6-8 minutes. While this is cooking, crack the eggs into the stirred rapidly boiling water, and poach for 2-3 minutes. In another medium pan, quickly wilt the spinach in only the water clinging to the leaves. Season.

4   Place the spinach, then the mash, on the plates. Drain the haddock and place on the mash. I spoon a little of the flavoured milk over this and top with a soft poached egg.

Grilled Aubergine with Tomato Sauce

Aubergines are not really English, but I'm growing them in my greenhouse and they taste wonderful. Simply pan-fry slices of aubergine, top with mozzarella cheese and Parmesan, place under the grill and serve with a tomato sauce. This is a real classic Italian dish that we Brits have learned to love.

Serves 4

plain white flour
4 medium eggs, beaten with a
    pinch of salt
2 aubergines, cut into 8mm ($^3/_8$ in)
    rounds
olive oil
salt and ground black pepper
300g (10$^1/_2$oz) buffalo mozzarella,
    sliced
100g (3$^1/_2$oz) Parmesan, grated

TOMATO AND BASIL SAUCE
extra virgin olive oil
1 medium onion, peeled and finely
    chopped
2 garlic cloves, peeled and finely
    chopped
1kg (2$^1/_4$lb) tomatoes, diced
$^1/_4$ tsp dried oregano
8 fresh basil leaves, torn

1   To make the sauce, heat 4 tbsp of olive oil in a pan and fry the onion and garlic for 4-5 minutes. Add the tomatoes and oregano, bring to the boil, then reduce the heat and cook for 10-15 minutes. Halfway through the cooking, add the basil leaves. Season and blend to a smooth sauce, then leave to one side.

2   Preheat 2 frying pans on the stove, and preheat the grill.

3   Put the flour and beaten eggs in separate shallow bowls. Dip the aubergine slices first in flour and then in beaten egg, and fry in shallow olive oil until golden on both side. Put each slice on absorbent paper.

4   Place the drained aubergine slices on a grill tray and season. Top with the sliced mozzarella and grated Parmesan.

5   Grill until the cheeses have melted and started to brown, then serve immediately with the heated tomato and basil sauce.

Honey-glazed Ham with Spiced Apple and Cider

I remember queuing up at Scotts Butchers as a kid with my gran and auntie. Armed with their handbags and pensions every Thursday, they would wait for dry-cured smoked back bacon and York ham. Sadly they don't do York ham any more, but if you're in York it's worth going to Scotts on Petergate to experience one of the greatest pork suppliers there is.

Serves 4-6

1 x 3.5kg (7.5lb) boiled ham,
   cooled
115g (4oz) clear honey
1 tbsp English mustard
finely grated zest and juice of
   1 orange
20 cloves

APPLE SAUCE
500g (1lb 2oz) Bramley Seedling
   apples
25g (1oz) butter
2 tbsp cider
¼ tsp freshly grated nutmeg
¼ tsp powdered cinnamon
¼ tsp freshly ground black pepper
25g (1 oz) soft dark brown sugar

1 Preheat the oven to 220°C/425°F/gas mark 7.

2 Score the ham fat diagonally at 2.5cm (1in) intervals, first in one direction, then another, to produce a diamond pattern.

3 Mix the honey, mustard, orange zest and enough orange juice to make a spreadable mixture. Smear this glaze over the ham. Stud the ham with the cloves at the points of the diamond shapes. Bake for 30 minutes, or until cooked through.

5 Meanwhile, for the sauce, peel, core and cut up the apples. Put them in a pan with all the remaining sauce ingredients apart from the sugar. Cover and cook until soft enough to beat to a purée. Add sugar to taste, and more spices if you like.

6 Serve the ham in slices, hot or cold, with the apple sauce.

Salmon with Beetroot, Cauliflower and Horseradish Cream

An odd dish, I know, but all the flavours work really well when eaten together. You can serve it all cold, but I like the vegetables cold and the salmon hot from the pan.

Serves 4

1 large cauliflower
juice of 1 lemon
4 tbsp horseradish cream
150ml (5fl oz) double cream, par-whipped
salt and freshly ground black pepper
4 x 115-175g (4-6oz) salmon fillets, skin on
olive oil

BEETROOT
8 medium beetroots, cooked
4 shallots, peeled and chopped
1 garlic clove, peeled and chopped
75ml (2½fl oz) extra virgin olive oil
10g (¼oz) mixed fresh chives, parsley and dill, chopped
2 tbsp balsamic vinegar

1   To prepare the beetroots, peel them, cut them into segments and place these in a bowl.

2   Sweat the shallots and garlic in a pan in a little of the oil, with no colour, then leave to cool. Mix with the herbs, balsamic and remaining oil, pour over the beetroot and leave to one side.

3   Divide the cauliflower into small florets and cook these in boiling water for about 5 minutes. When just cooked, plunge into iced water, drain and leave to one side.

4   Make the horseradish cream by combining the lemon juice and horseradish, then adding the par-whipped cream and some seasoning. Fold in the cauliflower and place in a serving bowl.

5   Season the salmon, then cook it in a hot pan in a little oil, for 3-4 minutes on both sides.

6   Serve the cold beetroot and cauliflower in separate containers on a plate, and the hot salmon on top of either one and the horseradish cream on the side.

Pan-fried Cod with Peas, Pancetta and Sweet Potato Crisp

This is probably the most cheffy recipe in the book, but it tastes great. The most important thing is to use a great cod fillet – thick white flesh with the skin still on – as this will help hold it together while cooking.

Serves 4

4 x 175-200g (6-7oz) thick pieces cod fillet, skin on
olive oil
salt and freshly ground black pepper
unsalted butter
200g (7oz) warm mashed potato (*see* page 143, omitting the horseradish)
8 slices pancetta, grilled until crisp
4 thin strips sweet potato, deep-fried

SAUCE
400ml (14fl oz) chicken stock
55g (2oz) pancetta, diced
15g (1oz) unsalted butter
1 small onion, peeled and finely chopped
2 garlic cloves, peeled and crushed
2 tbsp horseradish cream
a dash of white wine
150ml (5fl oz) double cream
350g (12oz) frozen peas
a pinch of caster sugar

1 Preheat the oven to 200°C/400°F/gas mark 6.

2 Start the sauce by reducing the stock. Boil until you have about 50ml (2fl oz) left.

3 Sauté the diced pancetta in the butter until crisp, then add the onion and garlic and soften without allowing them to colour. Add the horseradish, wine and reduced stock and simmer for a few minutes. Add the cream, peas and sugar, stir and season, and simmer for a few more minutes to heat the peas through.

4 Brush the cod fillets with olive oil, season and pan-fry for a minute on each side. Finish by cooking for 10 minutes in the oven, or until cooked,

5 Place the warm mash in the centre of the plates with the cod. Put a slice of crisp pancetta and a sweet-potato crisp on top, and spoon the sauce around.

Ginger and Butternut Squash Ice-cream

I know what you're thinking, squash in an ice-cream? Sounds weird, but trust me: I won't let you down. It really is a delight!

Serves 6

450ml (16fl oz) double cream
2 tbsp peeled and chopped fresh
    root ginger
4 medium egg yolks
100g (3½oz) caster sugar
ice
150g (5½oz) cooked, cooled and
    puréed butternut squash
a dash of lemon juice

1 Bring the cream and ginger to the boil together. Cover, remove from the heat and leave to steep for 30 minutes.

2 Return the cream to the boil. Whisk together the egg yolks and sugar in a jug and pour in some of the hot cream mixture. Mix quickly, then pour into the cream mixture left in the pan. Continue cooking over a gentle heat for 3-4 minutes, or until the mixture coats the back of the spoon. Cool over ice, stirring occasionally, until cold.

3 Mix the cooked and cooled squash purée into the cooled custard, add lemon juice to taste, and strain through a fine sieve. Freeze in an ice-cream machine or in a freezerproof container. Keep frozen until ready to use.

PARTIES, GIFTS AND TREATS

I love a wide variety of food at parties – from the traditional stuff like sausage rolls to crackers with some good cheese and a little onion marmalade to nibbles like home-made pork scratchings or spicy nuts. But of course the one thing no winter party should be without is a good glass of mulled wine!

Pork Scratchings

It's nice to offer your own scratchings with pre-dinner drinks, or you can even use them as a starter for a meal.

Makes as many as you like!

pork rind (preferably from the loin)
fine salt

1 Cut any excess fat from underneath the pork rind.

2 Preheat the oven to 200°C/400°F/gas mark 6.

3 Instead of scoring the rind, cut into 5mm (¼in) strips, then sprinkle with salt. Bake for 30-40 minutes (or longer for thicker pieces), until the pieces become crunchy.

Grissini and Dips

This is a quick and simple party idea, hardly a recipe, and it's good for a mobile starter to a dinner party, too

Makes as many as you like!

thin breadsticks or grissini
selection of dips, perhaps
   including garlic mayonnaise, soft
   cheese and tapenade
toasted sesame or poppy seeds or
   fresh herbs, finely chopped

1 Dip the ends of the breadsticks or grissini in the garlic mayonnaise, soft cheese or tapenade. Then dip the dipped end of the stick into the toasted seeds or herbs.

2 Serve, dipped end up, in tall glasses or in a large jug, so people can dive in and help themselves.

3 Alternatively, you can just wrap the grissini in some Parma ham, which makes a great snack as well.

Sausage Rolls

For me, party food wouldn't be party food without sausage rolls. I always look with horror at the rows and rows of sausage rolls and vol-au-vents stuffed with mushrooms and prawns with Marie Rose sauce at wedding buffets. There are no prawn vol-au-vents in this book and there won't ever be in any of my books, as I think they are the most repulsive things to ever hit the plate! However, sausage rolls when made right and served warm can be the finest delight England has to offer. You can use ordinary sausage-meat for these, either from a packet or meat taken out of the skins of your favourite sausages. But my favourite is wild boar sausage-meat, which makes a very special sausage roll!

Makes 16–20

450g (1lb) wild-boar sausage-meat
finely grated zest of ½ lemon
1 heaped tsp each of chopped
    fresh thyme and sage
salt and freshly ground black
    pepper
225g (8oz) ready-made puff pastry
plain flour
1 egg yolk mixed with 2 tsp milk

1   Preheat the oven to 200°C/400°F/gas mark 6.

2   Mix together the sausage-meat, lemon zest and chopped herbs. Season with salt and pepper. This can now be refrigerated, covered, to firm while the pastry is being rolled.

3   Roll the pastry to about 3mm (⅛in) thick on a floured surface. Cut into 3 long strips approximately 10cm (4in) wide.

4   The sausage-meat can now be moulded, using your hands, into 3 long sausages, preferably 2.5cm (1in) thick. If the meat is too moist, then dust it with flour.

5   Sit each "sausage" on a pastry strip, 2-3cm (¾-1¼in) from the edge of the pastry. Brush the pastry along the other side, close to the sausage, with the egg yolk and milk mixture. Fold the pastry over the meat, rolling it as you do so. When the pastry meets, leave a small overlap before cutting away any excess. Once rolled all along, lift them carefully, making sure that the seal is on the base when put down.

6   These can now be transferred to a greased baking sheet. The sausage rolls can be left as they are, or you can make 3-4 cuts with scissors along the top. Brush each with the remaining egg yolk before baking for 20-30 minutes.

7   Once baked golden and crispy, remove from the oven and serve the sausage rolls warm.

Baby Coffee Eclairs

This is the kind of party food that always impresses: delicious éclairs packed with thick pastry cream.

Makes 60–70 éclairs

1 quantity choux pastry (see opposite)
1 beaten egg

COFFEE PASTRY CREAM
300ml (1/2 pint) whole milk
10g (1/4oz) freshly ground coffee
4 large egg yolks
60g (2 1/4oz) unrefined caster sugar
60g (2 1/4oz) plain white flour, sifted
300ml (1/2 pint) double cream, lightly whipped

ICING
5 tsp instant coffee
3 tbsp boiling water
about 250g (9oz) fondant icing sugar

1 Preheat the oven to 220°C/425°F/gas mark 7. Lightly grease two baking sheets. Spoon the choux pastry into a large piping bag fitted with a 1.5cm (5/8in) nozzle. Pipe the pastry on the baking sheets into 4cm (1 3/4in) long éclairs. Brush with beaten egg and refine the shape at the same time. Bake for 15-20 minutes, or until well risen and golden.

2 Once the éclairs are fully formed and golden, turn the oven down to 160°C/ 325°/gas mark 3 and cook the éclairs for a further 5-10 minutes to dry them out until they are very crisp. The crisper they are, the easier they are to pipe and ice. Remove from the oven and cool completely – don't store them in an airtight container as this makes the pastry soggy.

3 Meanwhile, make the pastry cream: bring the milk and ground coffee to the boil in a pan, stirring all the time. Remove from the heat and leave to infuse for 10 minutes.

4 Meanwhile, whisk the egg yolks and sugar together. Add the flour and mix well. Strain the milk and coffee mixture through a fine sieve on to the egg and sugar mixture and stir well. Return to the pan and bring to the boil slowly, stirring all the time in a figure of eight so it doesn't catch. Once boiling, remove from the heat and pour into a clean bowl. Cover with cling film and leave to cool.

5 Whisk the cooled coffee pastry cream to loosen and break it down, then add the whipped cream and whisk together. Spoon into a piping bag fitted with a 5mm (1/4in) nozzle. Using a little knife, make small incisions in the base of each éclair large enough to fit the nozzle. Pipe the coffee cream into the éclairs one by one, until they feel heavy and full.

6 For the icing, mix together the instant coffee and boiling water, then gradually add enough fondant icing sugar to make an icing of coating consistency. Dip each éclair into the icing one at a time and smooth off with your finger. Leave to set for 15 minutes and then serve piled high.

Choux Pastry

Don't be put off making choux pastry by rumours of it being difficult. It's not that hard – honest – and well worth it!

Makes enough for about 70 baby éclairs

115g (4oz) unsalted butter, cubed
a pinch of sugar
a pinch of salt
140g (5oz) plain white flour, sifted
3-4 eggs, beaten

1 Bring the butter and 300ml (½ pint) of cold water to the boil in a pan. Add the sugar and salt, and then immediately add the flour and beat well until the mixture comes away from the pan. Allow to cool completely (more egg is absorbed when the mixture is cold).

2 Gradually add 3 of the beaten eggs to the cooled pastry, a little at a time (it's best to do this in a food mixer or food processor) and then beat small amounts of the last egg into the mixture until you get the right consistency. The reason for only adding 3 eggs at the start is that the mixture needs to be quite tight; if you add too much egg, the end product will not rise correctly and, of course, you can always add the extra egg but you can't take it out. If the paste is to be used for fritters or *beignets*, then it has to be fairly tight. The finished paste should just fall off the paddle on the machine. It's best to use choux dough straight away, but it will keep for a couple of days in the fridge.

Chocolate Truffles

Dark-chocolate truffles, like these, are the quickest and simplest to make. Milk and white chocolate truffles need different chocolate, as dark sets more solid – increase the amount by 115g (4oz). Mine are coated in cocoa powder. You can use icing sugar, coconut or grated chocolate, but if you do, roll the truffles in the coating while the chocolate is wet.

Makes 20-30

300ml (10fl oz) double cream
300g (10½oz) 70% dark chocolate
25ml (1fl oz) rum, brandy, etc.
   (optional)

COATING
200g (7oz) 70% dark chocolate,
   broken into small pieces
55g (2oz) good cocoa powder

1 Place the cream in a pan and heat until hot, but do not boil.

2 Break the chocolate into small even pieces and place in a bowl. When the cream is hot, pour it slowly on to the chocolate and, using a whisk, mix well until all the cream is combined and the chocolate has melted.

3 Before you set this mix, add any rum or brandy, if using, then leave it to set for about 2 hours in the fridge.

4 Using a melon scoop dipped in hot water, spoon the mixture into balls. Place them on a tray and put them back into the fridge.

5 Melt the chocolate for the coating in a bowl over a pan of hot water. Then stab each truffle with a fork, using it to dip the truffle in the chocolate and roll it in the cocoa. Place it on a plate and, once you have coated all the truffles, put them back in the fridge to set.

Fruit and Nut Biscotti

I end up making biscotti once a week because my PA devours half the jar every other week and the builders nick the rest. Biscotti are great biscuits that are easily made, and they can be stored in jars, given away as gifts, or even hung on the Christmas tree. Kids love them, as do adults, and my granny adored them.

Makes 40-50 biscotti

250g (9oz) plain flour
250g (9oz) caster sugar
$\frac{1}{2}$ tbsp baking powder
3 medium eggs, lightly beaten
55g (2oz) plump sultanas
55g (2oz) dried cherries
55g (2oz) pitted dates, chopped
75g (2^3/$_4$oz) shelled pistachio nuts
55g (2oz) whole blanched
  almonds
55g (2oz) shelled hazelnuts
finely grated zest of 1 lemon

1 Preheat the oven to 180°C/350°F/gas mark 4.

2 Mix the flour, sugar and baking powder in a large bowl. Add half the beaten eggs and mix well, then add half of what's left and mix again. Now add the last quarter a little bit at a time, mixing, until the dough takes shape but isn't too wet (you may not need to use all the egg). Add the fruit, nuts and lemon zest and mix well.

3 Divide the dough into six and roll each sixth into a sausage shape about 2.5cm (1in) in diameter. Place, at least 6cm (2$\frac{1}{2}$in) apart, on baking parchment on baking trays. Wetting your hands when rolling these out helps to prevent the dough sticking.

4 Lightly flatten the "sausages" and bake until golden brown, about 20-30 minutes. Remove from the oven and leave for 10 minutes to cool and firm up. Drop the temperature of the oven to 140°C/275°F/gas mark 1.

5 With a serrated knife, cut the biscotti on an angle into 5mm ($\frac{1}{4}$in) slices and lay these on the baking trays. Return to the oven and cook for 12 minutes. Turn the biscotti over and cook until they are pale golden, about 10-15 minutes.

6 When ready, remove from the oven and cool on cake racks. Store in airtight jars.

Onion Marmalade

This is bang in season around winter, and what could be better than a jar of onion marmalade given away as a gift? It goes brilliantly with melted cheese on toast, steak, roast fish, and a huge variety of other things, either hot or cold.

Makes 450g (1lb)

1.8kg (4lb) brown onions, peeled and thinly sliced
100ml (3½fl oz) olive oil
1 tbsp chopped fresh thyme
175g (6oz) caster sugar
150ml (5fl oz) red wine
6 tbsp red wine vinegar
salt and freshly ground black pepper

1   Place the onions in a large, heavy-based saucepan with the olive oil and thyme and cook over a moderate heat for 5 minutes. It is important not to let the onions brown at this stage or they will become bitter. Lower the heat, cover with a lid and cook for 20 minutes.

2   Remove the lid and add the sugar, wine, vinegar and some seasoning. Continue to cook, stirring from time to time, for about 20-30 minutes.

3   Once the jam is sticky, spoon it into sterilized jars. Lightly cover the surface with olive oil and put on the lids. Keep in a cool place until ready to use. Once opened, store in the fridge.

Index

almonds
    almond paste (marzipan) 108
    plum and almond tart 84
apples
    apple charlotte 69
    Bramley apple, custard and honey tart 85
    honey-glazed ham with spiced apple
     and cider 146
    in mint jelly 169
    toffee apples 98
apricots
    and pistachios with pork terrine 30
    sausage-meat, red pepper and apricot
     stuffing balls 132
aubergines
    grilled, with tomato sauce 144
    lamb, aubergine and watercress salad 12

bacon
    with Brussels sprouts and chestnuts 128
    with roast turkey 124
    with salt-baked baby potatoes and
     taleggio 90
    sausage and bacon wraps with sage
     and honey 134
    with scrambled eggs and chillies on
     toast 142
    in spicy bean stew with sausages 88
basil, tomato and basil sauce 144
beans
    broad, in a salad 10
    French, in a salad 10
    spicy bean stew with sausages 88
    tomato beans 38
beef
    burgers with soft onions 91
    fillet, with a prune and potato cake 26
    peppered roast beef 27
beetroot
    and mascarpone risotto 46
    with salmon, cauliflower and
     horseradish cream 148
bhajis, quick onion 51

biscotti, fruit and nut 166
bread
    bread sauce 133
    Christmas bread 112
    grissini and dips 156

cakes
    Christmas cake 106-8
    Gran's Madeira cake 113
    madeleines 168
    stollen 110
    yule log 114
cassis sauce 72
cauliflower, with salmon, beetroot and
  horseradish cream 148
cheese
    recipes with, *see* cream cheese;
     Emmental; mascarpone; mozzarella;
     Parmesan; Stilton; Vacherin
    cheese soufflé, double-baked 52
    cheese toasts with rich onion soup 18
chestnuts
    with Brussels sprouts and bacon 128
    stuffing 132
chicken, Thai chicken cakes with sweet
  chilli sauce 23
chillies
    with scrambled eggs and crisp streaky
     bacon 142
    sweet chilli jam 23
chocolate
    bitter chocolate tart 80
    chocolate and raspberry tarts with
     fennel 78
    and marron glacé tart 60
    quick chocolate tart 81
    truffles 162
    white chocolate and raspberry trifle 62
    yule log 114
choux pastry 160, 161
Christmas
    cake 106-8
    cooking 105-39

countdown to 120-1
dinner 124-39
chutneys, *see* pickles and chutneys
cod, pan-fried, with peas, pancetta and sweet
  potato crisp 149
coffee
    baby coffee éclairs 160
    coffee bean syrup 80
    coffee "mushrooms" 164
crab
    baked, with Parmesan crust 15
    sweetcorn and crab soup 20
cranachan 61
cranberries, spiced cranberry jelly 133
cream cheese, stuffing for roast turkey 126
croûtons, garlic croûtons 16
cumin, roast tomato and cumin soup 19
custard, Bramley apple, custard and
  honey tart 85

dauphinoise in a pan 54
dips 51, 156
dressings and vinaigrettes
    balsamic vinaigrette 12
    for bacon and bean salad 10
    for salad of char-grilled leeks 47
    for Yorkshire ham terrine 31
drinks
    bloody mary 142
    mulled wine 154
    sweet kir royale 154
duck
    duck liver paté with pear chutney 40
    honey-roast confit with tomato beans 38
    smoked, with melted Vacherin Mont
      d'Or and new potatoes 155

éclairs, baby coffee éclairs 160
eggs
    poached, with smoked haddock and
      horseradish mash 143
    scrambled, with chilli and crisp streaky
      bacon on toast 142

Emmental cheese, in double-baked
  soufflés 52

fennel
    with chocolate and raspberry tarts 78
    fennel oil 79
    grilled, with smoked haddock risotto 22
fish *see* cod; crab; mussels; smoked haddock
fondues, Stilton, with pear and walnut bread 52
frangipane 84

ginger, and butternut squash ice-cream 151
goose, roast, with stuffing 127
gravy, for Christmas turkey 124
grissini and dips 156

ham
    honey-glazed, with spiced apple and
      cider 146
    terrine, with spiced pickle 31
hangover cure, bloody mary 142
herb oil 94
horseradish
    cream 148
    mash 143

ice-cream
    baked, with Christmas pudding 138
    blood orange ice-cream 73
    cheat's raspberry and cassis ripple
      ice-cream 72
    Christmas pudding ice-cream 139
    ginger and butternut squash ice-cream 151
see also puddings
icing, royal icing 108

lamb, and aubergine and watercress
  salad 12
leeks, char-grilled, in a salad 47
lemons
    classic lemon posset 61
    and mustard with roast squash 92
    Sussex pond pudding 65

madeleines 168
marrons glacés
    chocolate and marron glacé tart 60
    festive 165
marshmallow 102
marzipan 108
mascarpone
    beetroot and mascarpone risotto 46
    with smoked haddock risotto 22
    in Stilton fondue 52
meat and game 25-40
mincemeat
    in real Christmas bread 112
    traditional 116
mint jelly 169
mozzarella
    with parsley croquettes 53
    in a salad with char-grilled leeks and
     red onions 47
mussel and saffron soup 16

New Year's Day food 141-51
nuts, hot spiced 155

onions
    caramelized 16
    with classic beef burgers 91
    onion marmalade 170
    quick onion bhajis 51
    red onion and crème fraiche tarts 44
    red onions in a salad with char-grilled
     leeks and mozzarella 47
    rich onion soup 18
oranges, blood orange ice-cream 73

pancakes, risen, with fresh fruit and maple
 syrup 71
pancetta, with pan-fried cod, peas and
 sweet potato crisp 149
Parmesan
    with baked crab 15
    with smoked haddock risotto 22
parsnips, roast 131

pastry
    choux pastry 160, 161
    puff pastry crusted pumpkin soup 95
    sweet shortcrust 76
paté, duck liver, with pear chutney 40
peas
    pea soup 20
    with smoked haddock risotto 22
pecan pie 82
peppers, sausage-meat, red pepper and
 apricot stuffing balls 132
pheasant, pot-roast, with cider and
 Calvados 34
pickles and chutneys
    pear chutney 40
    pineapple pickle 31
pine nuts, with butternut squash and
 lime soup 94
pistachios, and apricots with pork
 terrine 30
plum and almond tart 84
pork
    pork [sausage] terrine with apricots and
     pistachios 30
    scratchings 156
pot-roast, pheasant with cider and
 Calvados 34
potatoes
    dauphinoise in a pan 54
    horseradish mash 143
    new potatoes with melted Vacherin
     Mont d'Or and smoked duck 155
    parsley croquettes with mozzarella 53
    prune and potato cake with beef fillet 26
    roast potatoes 131
    salt-baked baby potatoes with taleggio
     and bacon 90
    prune and potato cake with beef fillet 26
puddings 57-73
    apple charlotte 69
    chocolate and marron glacé tart 60
    Christmas pudding 136
    cranachan 61

queen of puddings 70
quick Christmas pudding with baked
   ice-cream 138
risen pancakes with fresh fruit and
   maple syrup 71
Sussex pond pudding 65
syrup sponge with crushed raspberries 64
white chocolate and raspberry trifle 6
see also ice-cream
pumpkin, puff pastry crusted pumpkin
and rosemary soup 95

queen of puddings 70

raspberries
   cheat's raspberry and cassis ripple
      ice-cream 72
   chocolate and raspberry tarts with
      fennel 78
   syrup sponge with crushed raspberries 64
   white chocolate and raspberry trifle 62
rosemary, with puff pastry crusted pumpkin
   soup 95
royal icing 108

saffron, in smoked haddock risotto with
   peas and grilled fennel 22
salads
   bacon and bean 10
   char-grilled leeks, red onions and
      mozzarella 47
   lamb, aubergine and watercress 12
   with pork terrine with apricots and
      pistachios 30
salmon, with beetroot and cauliflower and
   horseradish cream 148
sauces
   apple 146
   brandy 139
   cassis 72
   for cheese soufflé 52
   home-made tomato ketchup 91
   mint jelly 169

onion marmalade 170
for pan-fried cod 149
red wine 26, 38
sweet chilli jam 23
tomato and basil 144
sausage rolls 158
sausage-meat
   red pepper and apricot stuffing balls 132
   stuffing 127
sausages
   in pork terrine with apricots and
      pistachios 30
   sausage and bacon wraps with sage
      and honey 134
spicy bean stew with sausages 88
shallots, tarte tatin 50
shellfish *see* crab; mussels
smoked haddock
   with poached egg and horseradish
      mash 143
   risotto with saffron, peas and grilled
      fennel 22
soups
   butternut squash and lime soup with pine
      nuts and herb oil 94
   mussel and saffron soup, with caramelized
      onions 16
   pea soup 20
   puff pastry crusted pumpkin and
      rosemary soup 95
   rich onion soup, with cheese toast 18
   roast tomato and cumin soup 19
   sweetcorn and crab soup 20
sprouts, Brussels sprouts with chestnuts
   and bacon 128
squash
   butternut squash and lime soup with
      pine nuts and herb oil 94
   ginger and butternut squash
      ice-cream 151
   roast squash, with lemon and mustard 92
starters 9-23
stews, spicy bean, with sausages 88

Stilton fondue, with pear and walnut
  bread 52
stollen 110
Sussex pond pudding 65
sweet potato, with pan-fried cod, peas and
  pancetta 149
sweetcorn and crab soup 20
syrups, coffee bean 80

taleggio, with salt-baked baby potatoes
  and bacon 90
tarte tatin, with shallots 50
tarts 75-85
    bitter chocolate 80
    Bramley apple, custard and honey 85
    chocolate and marron glacé 60
    chocolate and raspberry with fennel 78
    pecan pie 82
    plum and almond 84
    quick chocolate 81
    red onion and crème fraiche 44
terrines
    pork with apricots and pistachios 30
    Yorkshire ham with spiced pickle 31

Thai chicken cakes with sweet chilli
  sauce 23
toffee apples 98
tomatoes
    home-made tomato ketchup 91
    roast tomato and cumin soup 19
    tomato and basil sauce 144
    tomato beans 38
treacle toffee 98
turkey
    with orange, rosemary and gravy 124
    roast, stuffed with cream cheese and
      herbs 126

Vacherin Mont d'Or, melted, with new
  potatoes and smoked duck 155
vanilla sugar 165
vegetables 43-54
    roasted, with rosemary and honey 48
vinaigrettes *see* dressings and vinaigrettes

watercress salad 12

Yorkshire pudding 27

Acknowledgements

Thanks to Simon, Catherine, Karen and Nicky for a great shoot!